JN102671

English for Exploring the World
Developing Communication Skills

Koji Uenishi

Walter Davies

Simon Fraser

Julia Tanabe

Daniel Hougham

＊音声のトラックナンバーについて＊

マークの中にあるナンバーは、それぞれ次の のトラックを意味しています。

数字の前に S があるナンバーは付属（学生用）

数字の前に T があるナンバーは教授用

EIHŌSHA

Dedication

We would like to dedicate this book to Keiko Uenishi, Hideko Tetsui, Rie Fraser, Hiromasa Tanabe, and Mayumi Hougham in gratitude for their patience and help during the time it took to write this book.

Authors' Acknowledgements

In creating the textbook and the listenings, we received a great deal of advice and support. We would particularly like to thank the following individuals and institutions:

Fuyuko Takita, Goro Yamamoto, Axel Harting, Katherine Song, Joe Lauer, Peter Howell, Jaime Selwood, Kumiko Fujiwara, Misa Kurokawa, Yuki Yamasawa, Claude Lévi Alvarès, Pornnapa Lévi Alvarès, Dararat Kakizono, Hans-Michael Schlarb, Carolin Funck, Jon Clenton, Robert Taferner, Wei Wang, Dion Clingwall, Aaron C. Sponseller, Jean-Gabriel Santoni, Akimasa Fujiwara, Deepak Kumar, Sushil Bapurao Raut, Jingxian Li

The Museum of Flight, Seattle
The Langenbeck-Virchow House, Berlin

In the textbook, timetables, prices, menus, and other items, while roughly based on real-world situations, have been created or adapted so that students can practice extracting key information. The self-study scripts use data from 2023.

All errors and inaccuracies are the authors' own.

About this book

English for Exploring the World is a textbook that is specifically designed for young Japanese adults at pre-intermediate and intermediate levels. The book follows the journeys of two Japanese university students, Yuta and Hana, as they travel around the world, exploring aspects of different cultures and histories. Each unit is set in a country in Europe (the UK, France, and Germany), North America (the USA and Canada), or Asia (Singapore, India, Thailand, and China).

Learners are presented with the language necessary for them to handle a wide variety of conversational situations. There is a particular focus on solving problems that they might encounter while using English. Each unit is organized so that learners can practice in both a controlled way and in freer situations where they can draw widely on their English language skills. The book features tasks designed to enhance speaking and listening, but students are also provided with opportunities for developing their writing and vocabulary. Useful language for traveling and problem-solving is combined with opportunities to explore culture. Each main unit consists of six pages, and is divided into nine main parts:

Warm up uses photographs and questions to set the scene for each unit and activate learners' existing knowledge of the country and situations they will encounter in the unit.

Dialogue practice focuses on listening skills, and contains two conversations which present the communicative language of the unit in context. These conversations provide opportunities for controlled speaking practice.

Vocabulary check is a definition-matching exercise which helps consolidate the key vocabulary of the unit.

Role play provides learners with an opportunity to develop and practice the language they have learned in a less structured and more creative way.

Key expression focuses on an important example of the functional language introduced in the dialogues, and provides learners with practice in using the expression in a variety of situations.

Dialogue writing gives learners the opportunity to further demonstrate their creativity by writing and performing a short skit covering the key language introduced in the unit.

Discussion provides learners with further listening practice, and gives them a chance to share their opinions and viewpoints on a variety of issues related to the content of the unit.

Online research task gives learners the opportunity to find out more about the culture of the unit's location and to present what they have found.

Self-study can be done as a homework assignment. It has a listening-based task that focuses on interesting aspects of the culture of each of the countries introduced in the units, including art, history, and politics. The section also includes a set of questions giving learners a chance to review the language, functions, and concepts presented in the unit.

In addition to the main units, the book also contains a short introductory unit about travel and Japan. This is designed to encourage students to think about their own travel experiences and Japanese culture before exploring the locations in the rest of the book. There are also two review units, one after Unit 6 and one after Unit 12, which are designed to help learners review and reflect on what they have studied.

Audio recordings can be downloaded at https://www.eihosha.co.jp/. Online supplementary material featuring flashcards, games, and tests are available on Quizlet (https://quizlet.com).

We have designed this course to be helpful, informative, and enjoyable. We hope that you have fun using English to explore the world with Yuta and Hana.

Koji Uenishi, Walter Davies, Simon Fraser, Julia Tanabe, and Daniel Hougham

Quizlet: AI-Powered Flashcards to Boost Your Vocabulary

How to Use Quizlet:
Step 1: Scan the QR code.
Step 2: Choose the unit from our textbook you want to study.
Step 3: Start learning via self-study flashcards, games, or tests.
Enjoy learning with AI-powered Quizlet!
https://quizlet.com/eihosha/folders/english-for-exploring-the-world/sets

Get the app to study anytime, anywhere! Scan the QR code to download the app (https://quizlet.com/mobile)

Table of Contents

Introduction

In this introductory unit, you are going to:
- talk about travel and your own experiences
- think about culture and famous sites in Japan

Travel

Work in pairs. Look at the different types of transportation in the pictures. Which of these have you used recently and why? What other ones do you use?

Example

A I used a local train yesterday.

B Where did you go?

A I always use the local train to come here.

Talk to your classmates. Find people who answer "Yes" to a question and then get more information.

Example

A Do you want to visit North America?

B Yes, I do.

A Which part?

B I've always wanted to visit Vancouver.

	Name	Notes
Find someone who...		
1. ... has been to Kyoto.		
2. ... wants to visit North America.		
3. ... wants to visit Europe.		
4. ... has been to Miyajima.		
5. ... uses a train regularly.		
6. ... has traveled by plane.		
7. ... has visited another country in Asia.		
8. ... is planning to travel somewhere soon.		
9. ... (your idea)_____.		

In Japan

Work with another student. Ask and answer the following questions.

1. What places can you see in the two pictures?
2. What would you tell someone about each place?
3. What's your favorite place to go sightseeing in Japan?
4. What are the best places to see in your local area?
5. What are Japan's most famous dishes?

Planning a trip in Japan

Work with another student. Imagine that you have a visitor from Canada. Plan a five-day trip around Japan. Decide what transportation you will use, what you will do there, and what you will eat.

Notes
Day 1:
Day 2:
Day 3:
Day 4:
Day 5:

Unit 1: Traveling by plane

> **In this unit, you are going to:**
> - study and practice some airport and plane conversations
> - practice *"If I were you, I'd ..."*
> - discuss airplane travel
> - research Singapore

Warm up

Work with another student. Ask and answer the following questions.

1. Describe the photographs.
2. What would you like to know about Singapore?
3. What places have you visited recently, either in Japan or overseas, and how did you get there?
4. What is your favorite kind of transportation, and why?

Plane ticket

✈ booking reference

Reservation Number		Date	Name of Passenger/s
KS4HDN	‖‖‖‖‖‖	07 Feb 20××	MR Yuta Tanaka

Name   Yuta Tanaka
Address   1-12-15 Otemachi
                Naka-ku
                Hiroshima
                725-6813

✈ your itinerary

Date	Flight Number	Departing	Arriving
Mon 14 May 20××	SGP 5371	SINGAPORE 1030 hr	AMSTERDAM 1730 hr
	SGP 2361	AMSTERDAM 1830 hr	LONDON 1845

All times indicated are the local times at the relevant airport.   ** Fare rules on following page.*

Reminder: This Booking is non-refundable. Cancellations at any time or failure to check-in for a Valuair flight at least 40 minutes before the scheduled departure will result in the fare being forfeited.

A printed copy of this itinerary must be produced during check in.

Look at the e-ticket and answer the following questions.

1. What is the passenger's first name?
2. Where does he live?
3. On what date is he traveling?
4. What is his final destination?
5. Where does he have to change planes?

Dialogue: Checking in

Listen to the conversation and fill in the blanks.

At the check-in desk.

Clerk Could I see your passport and e-ticket, please?

  Yuta Here you are.

Clerk Thank you. Are you going to London?

  Yuta Yes, I am.

Clerk And you'll need to transfer planes in Amsterdam.

  Yuta Yes, that's right.

Clerk (1)_____?

  Yuta Yes, I did.

Clerk Are there any of the items in this picture in your suitcase?

  Yuta I don't think so .... No, there aren't.

Clerk OK, I'll find a seat for you.

  Yuta (2)_____, please?

Clerk I'm sorry, but the flight is very busy today. There are only some middle seats left.

  Yuta Oh, OK.

Clerk So ... (3)_____ from Singapore. You need to go to gate 22. This other one is for your Amsterdam – London flight. (4)_____. Have a good flight.

  Yuta Thank you.

Now practice the conversation with another student.

Dialogue: Lunch on the plane

Listen to the dialogue and answer the following questions.

1. What does Yuta order at lunchtime?
2. What problem does he have?
3. How does the passenger next to him usually check in?
4. What is the main reason for Yuta's trip to the UK?

On the plane. About an hour after take-off, flight attendants begin serving meals to passengers.

Attendant Which would you prefer, fish or meat?

    Yuta Umm .... What's the meat and what's the fish?

Attendant Chicken and salmon.

    Yuta I'll have the salmon, please.

Attendant Here you are. And what would you like to drink, sir?

    Yuta Just water, please. .... Thanks.

As Yuta is trying to eat his fish in the cramped space, his knife slips and he knocks over some water. Some of it splashes onto his neighbor's leg.

    Yuta Oh, I'm sorry!

Passenger It's OK. You've got water all over your tray table. Here, take my napkin. I'll call the attendant.

    Yuta Thanks.

Attendant Are you OK?

    Yuta I've spilled some water. Could you bring some paper towels?

Attendant I'll be right back, sir. .... Here you are.

    Yuta Thanks.

Yuta turns to speak to the neighboring passenger.

    Yuta I'm so sorry about this.

Passenger It's OK. There's not much space to eat, is there?

    Yuta No, there isn't! I was hoping for an aisle seat but there weren't any left this morning.

Passenger I do this journey once or twice a year and the plane is always crowded. <u>If I were you, I'd</u> check in on the internet next time. I find I can always get a window seat that way. Do you live in Singapore?

    Yuta No, I'm from Japan. I'm a student and I've just attended a conference in Singapore.

Passenger So, where are you going today?

    Yuta I'm on my way to a summer course in Edinburgh, and I want to do some sightseeing in London before going on the course. I got this flight because I want to see Amsterdam on my way back to Japan.

Passenger Oh, I'm heading for London, too. I live in Singapore, but I usually go to the UK for my summer vacation.

    Yuta Are there any places you recommend in London? ....

Now practice the conversation with another student.

Vocabulary check

Read each definition and write down the correct word.

> 1. a formal meeting of people with a shared interest: c_____
> 2. filled with a large number of people: c_____
> 3. a small piece of cloth or paper used when eating: n_____
> 4. to let fall or cause to fall from a container: s_____
> 5. the space between rows of seats: a_____
> 6. to tell a person that something is good or useful: r_____

Role play

Read through the dialogues. Then close your books and act out the situations.
A: Yuta Tanaka
B: clerk, flight attendant, neighboring passenger

Key expression: *If I were you, I'd ...*

  Yuta: I was hoping for an aisle seat but there weren't any left this morning.
Passenger: If I were you, I'd check in on the internet next time.

Work with another student. Listen to the problem and give advice.

Example
 A: I forgot to do my homework last night.
 B: If I were you, I'd ask the teacher if you could bring it next week.

Student A
 1. I forgot to buy a birthday present for my friend.
 3. I'm putting on weight.
 5. I haven't been able to eat for three days because of stomach pains.

Student B
 2. I don't have enough money to cover my living costs.
 4. I lost my wallet in the cafeteria yesterday.
 6. I can't get up in the mornings, so I'm often late for class.

Dialogue writing

Work with another student. Choose one of the problems on page 9 and prepare a short skit between two students, Emi and John, who meet each other on campus. Use the "notes" pages at the back of the book. Start with the following:

> **John:** Hi Emi. How are you?
>
> **Emi:** Hi John. Fine, thanks. You look worried. What's wrong?
>
> **John:**

Practice the dialogue with your partner.
Close your book and practice the skit from memory.

Discussion

Work with another student. Ask and answer the following questions.

> 1. Do you like traveling? Why or why not?
> 2. If you spilled a whole glass of orange juice over someone, what would you do?
> 3. What problems have you had while traveling and how did you solve them?
> 4. If you could travel anywhere, where would you like to go, and why?
> 5. How would you spend your time on a long plane journey?
> 6. Which do you prefer, a window seat or an aisle seat, and why?

Online research task

Work in a small group. Do an internet search to find out about Singapore. Choose a famous sightseeing spot that interests you.

- *Watch a YouTube video about it.*
- *Use Google Maps and an online encyclopedia to learn more.*
- *Make notes about three things you learned, and share them with another group. Answer their questions using the internet if necessary.*

> ***Example***   We researched *Marina Bay Sands. It's a big resort hotel with three towers.* Three things we learned about it are: *(1) It has 2,561 hotel rooms, (2) there is a 150-meter infinity swimming pool in the Skypark, and (3) there is an ArtScience Museum building shaped like a lotus flower.*

Self-study
Singapore

Match the words to the definitions.

1. republic___	a) to change a damaged object back into good condition
2. trading post___	b) a large platform used for removing oil from under the sea
3. hub___	c) the process of improving something
4. port___	d) a country without a king, queen, or emperor
5. refining___	e) an area next to the sea where ships can stop
6. oil rig___	f) a place where goods can be bought or sold
7. repair___	g) a central area of activity, connected to many other areas

Listen to the recording and write the answers.

1. What is the English meaning of the name "Singapore"?
2. What is the population of Singapore?
3. How many official languages are there?
4. Why did Stamford Raffles create a trading post on the island?
5. When did Singapore become an independent republic?
6. In what ways is Singapore a commercial hub?

Dialogue review

Read through the unit and answer the following questions.

1. What kind of seat did Yuta want?
2. What kind of seat did he get?
3. What was the final destination on the ticket?
4. Did Yuta choose meat or fish for his meal?
5. What did Yuta spill?
6. What did the flight attendant bring?

Unit 2: Buying a train ticket

> ***In this unit, you are going to:***
> - study and practice some hotel and station conversations
> - practice *"Excuse me. Where can I ...?"*
> - discuss tourist sites and how to get to them
> - research London

Warm up

Work with another student. Ask and answer the following questions.

1. Describe the photographs.
2. When was the last time you stayed in a hotel? Where was it, and why did you stay there?
3. Which do you prefer, a modern room with a bed or a traditional room with a futon?
4. Do you like visiting big cities like London and Tokyo? Why or why not?

Online train schedules

								Return tickets
Dep	From	To	Arr.	Dur.	Chg.		Status	Fare
10:00	London Kings Cross [KGX]	Edinburgh [EDB]	14:22	4h 22m	0	Details	✓	£126.70 off peak
11:00	London Kings Cross [KGX]	Edinburgh [EDB]	15:21	4h 21m	0	Details	✓	£126.70 off peak
11:21	London Kings Cross [KGX]	Edinburgh [EDB]	16:05	4h 44m	1	Details	✓	£126.70 off peak
11:30	London Kings Cross [KGX]	Edinburgh [EDB]	16:14	4h 44m	0	Details	✓	£126.70 off peak
12:00	London Kings Cross [KGX]	Edinburgh [EDB]	16:23	4h 23m	0	Details	✓	£126.70 off peak

Look at the internet site and answer the following questions.

1. How much does a return ticket to Edinburgh cost?
2. Which London station do the trains leave from?
3. If Yuta wants the shortest traveling time, which train should he take?
4. What is the disadvantage of catching the 11:21 train?

Dialogue: **In the hotel**

Listen to the conversation and fill in the blanks.

At the hotel information desk.
Concierge Good morning, sir.
Yuta Good morning. (1) _____ ?
Concierge Certainly, sir. What's the destination and the day?
Yuta I'm going to Edinburgh tomorrow.
Concierge OK, I'll check the times on the internet. (2) _____ _____ ?
Yuta I'm not sure. I want to visit the British Museum for about an hour.
Concierge Well, that opens at 10:00. Are you sure you only need an hour there?
Yuta Yes, there are just a few things I want to see.
Concierge There are trains to Edinburgh leaving at 11:30 and 12:00 from King's Cross, which is only five minutes' walk from here.
Yuta (3) _____ ?
Concierge At 4:23 in the afternoon.
Yuta Do you think I can make the train if I finish at the British Museum around 11:00?
Concierge You should be OK. However, (4) _____ _____. It's usually cheaper if you pick a train time.
Yuta I'll go and buy one now. And can I leave my suitcase at the hotel tomorrow after I check out?
Concierge Sure. If you ask the receptionists tomorrow, (5) _____ _____ until you pick it up.
Yuta That's great. Thank you.
Concierge You're welcome.

Now practice the conversation with another student.

Dialogue: **At the station**

Listen to the dialogue and answer the following questions.

1. Why can't Yuta use the machines?
2. Where is the ticket office?
3. What will Yuta have to do if he doesn't take the 12:00 train?
4. Where is the reserved seat?

At the entrance to King's Cross station. The station is large and crowded. Yuta approaches a railway employee.

<blockquote>

Yuta <u>Excuse me. Where can I</u> buy a ticket?

Rail employee 1 There are some machines over there.

Yuta I'm sorry. I didn't catch that. Ma ...?

Rail employee 1 Look over there. Do you see the sign?

Yuta "Self service"?

Rail employee 1 Yes, you can buy a ticket at one of those machines.

Yuta Ah, I see ... *machines*. Actually, I want to talk to someone.

Rail employee 1 Oh, OK. In that case, walk past those machines and you'll get to the ticket office.

Yuta Thank you.

</blockquote>

At the ticket office.

<blockquote>

Yuta I want to buy a return ticket to Edinburgh for tomorrow.

Rail employee 2 Are you traveling in the morning or the afternoon?

Yuta I want to catch the 12:00 train. What's your cheapest ticket?

Rail employee 2 It's £126.70, but you have to catch that train. If you take a different one, you'll be charged extra.

Yuta That's fine.

Rail employee 2 OK. That's £126.70, please.

Yuta Here you are.

Rail employee 2 Here's the ticket and the reservation. Your reserved seat is 2A in car 3.

Yuta Thank you. And where can I get a map of the Underground?

Rail employee 2 There are some Tube maps over there by the wall.

Yuta I'm sorry. I don't understand. I want a map of the Underground.

Rail employee 2 The Tube *is* the Underground. The maps are over there.

Yuta Oh, I see. Thank you.

</blockquote>

Now practice the conversation with another student.

Vocabulary check

Read each definition and write down the correct word.

1. a piece of mechanical or electronic equipment: m_____
2. a situation where you serve yourself: s_____ s_____
3. a document for traveling to a place and back again: r_____ t_____
4. an arrangement to keep a seat for someone: r_____
5. a train system that runs beneath a city (British English): u_____
6. the name of the train system beneath London: the T_____

Role play

Read through the dialogues. Then close your books and act out the situations.

A: Yuta Tanaka

B: concierge, railway employee 1, railway employee 2

Key expression: *Excuse me. Where can I ...?*

        Yuta: Excuse me. Where can I buy a ticket?

Rail employee: There are some machines over there.

Work with another student. Listen to the question and give advice.

Example

A: Excuse me. Where can I buy a magazine around here?

B: There's a convenience store next to the entrance of the university.

Student A

1. ... buy a magazine?
3. ... make a photocopy?
5. ... get a cup of coffee?

Student B

2. ... catch a bus?
4. ... get a bottle of water?
6. ... use a computer?

Dialogue writing

Work with another student. Use the key expression on page 15 to write a short skit between a student and a visitor to the campus. Use the "notes" pages at the back of the book. Start with the following:

Visitor: *Excuse me. Could you help me?*

  Seiji: *Sure.*

Visitor:

Practice the dialogue with your partner.
Close your book and practice the skit from memory.

Discussion

T 06

Work with another student. Ask and answer the following questions.

1. What is the best tourist site in this prefecture?
2. What's the easiest way to get to it?
3. What would you do if you lost your way?
4. What do you usually do if you don't understand what someone is saying?
5. What is the best way of traveling round a big city like Tokyo?
6. Which do you prefer, buses or trains, and why?

Online research task

Work in a small group. Do an internet search to find out about London. Choose a famous sightseeing spot that interests you.
- *Watch a YouTube video about it.*
- *Use Google Maps and an online encyclopedia to learn more.*
- *Make notes about three things you learned, and share them with another group. Answer their questions using the internet if necessary.*

Example We researched *King's Cross station*. We learned three things: *(1) The station was opened in 1852, (2) it is one of the busiest stations in the UK, and (3) it is associated with the Harry Potter stories because of the fictional platform 9³/⁴.*

Self-study
London and the Greenwich Observatory

Match the words to the definitions.

1. observatory___	a) an imaginary line from the North Pole to the South Pole
2. longitude___	b) main or most important
3. astronomical___	c) a very accurate clock
4. navigation___	d) the distance of a place east or west of a key north-south line
5. prime___	e) connected with the observation of objects such as stars
6. meridian___	f) a building from which scientists can watch the sky
7. chronometer___	g) finding the way from one place to another

Listen to the recording and write the answers.   S 27

1. When was the Royal Observatory founded?
2. Why was the Royal Observatory built?
3. What was the problem of longitude?
4. What did the British parliament offer in 1714?
5. What did John Harrison make?
6. What is the longitude of the Greenwich Meridian?

Dialogue review

Read through the unit and answer the following questions.

1. What tourist site did Yuta want to visit?
2. How far was his hotel from King's Cross station?
3. Why didn't Yuta want to use the ticket machines?
4. What kind of ticket did Yuta buy?
5. How much did the ticket cost?
6. What is another name for the London Underground?

Unit 3: Accommodation and food

Warm up

Work with another student. Ask and answer the following questions.

1. Describe the photographs.
2. Would you like to stay in a student dormitory overseas? Why or why not?
3. When was the last time you went to a café or restaurant? What did you eat or drink there?
4. How would you describe an *izakaya* to a foreign tourist?

Information about a hall of residence (student dormitory)

Fraser Court	
Features	
Catering	No. Self-catered flats with shared kitchen
Laundry	Yes, coin-operated or electronic payment
Wi-Fi & Telephone	Yes, further details below
Car Parking	Restricted, on request only
Cycle Storage	Yes
Contents Insurance	Yes
Electricity & Heating included	Yes
Smoking	All our properties are non-smoking

Answer the questions about the Fraser Court hall of residence.

1. Can you smoke in Fraser Court?
2. Is there a cafeteria in Fraser Court?
3. If you want to park a car at Fraser Court, what do you have to do?
4. How can you pay when you wash your clothes?

Dialogue: At the reception center for university accommodation

Listen to the conversation and fill in the blanks.

S 06 ○ T 07

> *At the reception center.*
> **Receptionist** Good evening, sir.
> **Yuta** Good evening. I'm here for a four-week English course, and (1)__
>   _____ in university accommodation.
> **Receptionist** May I have your name, sir?
> **Yuta** Yes, it's Yuta Tanaka.
> **Receptionist** OK, let me just check. Here it is. Yuta Tanaka. You've reserved a
>   single room in Fraser Court?
> **Yuta** Yes, that's right.
> **Receptionist** I need your credit card details now, but (2)_____.
>   Is that OK?
> **Yuta** That's fine.
> **Receptionist** Please put your card in the machine. One moment. (3)_____
>   _____.
> **Yuta** My pen? Do I need to sign?
> **Receptionist** No, no. Just type in the number for your card.
> **Yuta** Oh, I see ....
> *Yuta types in his PIN.*
> **Receptionist** That's fine. Your card has been accepted. Here are your keys. If
>   you look at this map, we're here and Fraser Court is just round
>   the corner. There are two keys. (4)_____
>   and this one is your room key.
> **Yuta** Thank you. By the way, is there somewhere to eat near here?
> **Receptionist** The best place is the King's Arms, which is a pub about three
>   minutes' walk from Fraser Court. (5)_____.
> **Yuta** Great. Thanks a lot!
> **Receptionist** No problem. Enjoy your stay in Edinburgh!

Now practice the conversation with another student.

Dialogue: At the pub

S 07 ○ T 08

Listen to the dialogue and answer the following questions.

1. What kind of beer is "Belhaven"?
2. What is "haggis"?
3. What food does Yuta order?
4. What is the difference in value between a Scottish pound and a Bank of England pound?

In the King's Arms pub, Yuta goes up to the bar.

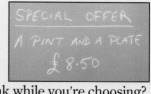

Publican Good evening. What can I get you?

  Yuta I'd like to order some food and a drink. How do I do that?

Publican You order here at the bar. The food menu is on the blackboard. What would you like to drink while you're choosing?

  Yuta Can I have a glass of beer?

Publican Certainly. I just need to check you're over eighteen. Could you show me some ID?

  Yuta Sure. I'm twenty-one. Here's my passport.

Publican That's great. Which beer would you like? We've got lagers, bitters, Guinness ...

  Yuta Umm ... there are so many. What do you recommend?

Publican The Belhaven is very good.

  Yuta What kind of beer is it?

Publican It's a bitter beer, brewed here in Scotland.

  Yuta OK, I'll try it.

Publican A pint or a half?

  Yuta I'm sorry, I don't understand.

Publican A large glass or a small one?

  Yuta Large, please.

Publican A pint. And what food would you like?

  Yuta What is "haggis, neeps, and tatties"?

Publican Haggis, turnip, and potatoes. It's a very traditional Scottish dish.

  Yuta What's "haggis"?

Publican It's the heart, liver, and lungs of a sheep minced with onion and spices inside a sheep's stomach, but nowadays a sausage casing is used. It tastes better than it sounds!

  Yuta Umm ... maybe I'll try it tomorrow. I'll have the fish and chips.

Publican OK. What's your table number?

  Yuta Oh, I don't have one.

Publican In this pub, the tables have numbers, and you should find a table and then order food. Look, that table over there is free. It's number four. If you sit there, I'll bring the food over when it's ready.

  Yuta Thank you.

Publican Here's your Belhaven. In total that comes to eight pounds fifty.

Yuta hands him a twenty pound note and the publican gives him the change.

  Yuta Excuse me. What's this note?

Publican It's a Scottish ten pound note.

  Yuta What's the difference between this one and my ten pound notes?

Publican You have Bank of England notes, but they're all the same value. The only difference is ours are prettier!

  Yuta Oh, I see! Thank you very much.

Publican You're welcome. Enjoy the Belhaven!

Now practice the conversation with another student.

Vocabulary check

Read each definition and write down the correct word.

1. to make beer: b_____
2. an amount of liquid equal to about half a liter: p_____
3. a traditional Scottish dish made from parts of a sheep: h_____
4. the name of French fries in the UK: ch_____
5. body organs that are used for breathing: l_____
6. how much something is worth: v_____

Role play

Read through the dialogues. Then close your books and act out the situations.

A: Yuta Tanaka

B: receptionist, publican

Key expression: *What _____ do you recommend?*

     Yuta: Can I have a glass of beer?

Publican: Which one? We've got lagers, bitters, Guinness ...

     Yuta: Umm ... there are so many. What do you recommend?

Publican: The Belhaven is very good.

Work with a partner. Listen to the question and give a recommendation.

Example

A: What Japanese beer do you recommend?

B: Asahi Super Dry is very good.

A: What do you like about it?

B: Well, it's really tasty and refreshing.

Student A

1. J-pop singer or group
3. make of computer (e.g., Fujitsu, Apple)
5. recent movie

Student B

2. smartphone provider (e.g., Softbank, Docomo)
4. local restaurant
6. comic (*manga*) or magazine

Dialogue writing

Work with a partner. Use the key expression on page 21 to write a short skit between a foreign visitor and a waitress in an izakaya. Use the "notes" pages at the back of the book. Start with the following:

Waitress: Irrashaimase!

   Visitor: *Good evening.*

Waitress: *Good evening. Welcome to our restaurant.*

Practice the dialogue with your partner.
Close your book and practice the skit from memory.

Discussion

Work with another student. Ask and answer the questions.

1. Where would you like to study overseas?
2. What are the advantages and disadvantages of doing a short language course during the vacation?
3. Explain some of the following: haggis, bagpipes, Arthur Conan Doyle, Adam Smith, tartan, Robert Burns, Scotch, Nessie.
4. In what way is an izakaya different from the pub that Yuta visited?
5. What Japanese dishes would you recommend to a foreign visitor, and why?
6. Which famous people are on the 1,000 yen, 5,000 yen, and 10,000 yen notes? Can you explain why they are famous?

Online research task

Work in a small group. Do an internet search to find out about Edinburgh. Choose a famous sightseeing spot that interests you.
  - *Watch a YouTube video about it.*
  - *Use Google Maps and an online encyclopedia to learn more.*
  - *Make notes about three things you learned, and share them with another group. Answer their questions using the internet if necessary.*

Example We researched *Edinburgh Castle*. We learned three things: *(1) It is built on an extinct volcano, (2) St Mary's Chapel in the castle is one of Scotland's oldest buildings, and (3) during its history, the castle has been besieged (attacked) 23 times.*

Self-study

Edinburgh and the Enlightenment

Match the words to the definitions.

1. century___	a) the general opinion that is held about someone or something
2. reputation___	b) concerning good or bad behavior, fairness, honesty, etc.
3. period___	c) businesses relating to money and investments
4. economy___	d) an organized set of special events, such as musical performances
5. moral___	e) the system of trade and industry by which the wealth of a country is made and used
6. financial services___	f) a 100-year length of time
7. festival___	g) a length of time identified by its culture, e.g., "Meiji"

Listen to the recording and write the answers.

1. What is the population of Edinburgh?
2. Why was the city called "The Athens of the North"?
3. What was the name of the period of reason and science in the eighteenth century?
4. What is Adam Smith often called?
5. What are Adam Smith's two most famous works?
6. What happens in August every year in Edinburgh?

Dialogue review

Read through the unit and answer the following questions.

1. Why did Yuta go to Edinburgh?
2. What was the name of his hall of residence?
3. Where did he go to eat?
4. What size beer did he order?
5. How much change did he get?
6. What was the number of his table?

Unit 4: Doing a homestay

Warm up

Work with another student. Ask and answer the following questions.

1. Describe the photographs.
2. What do you know about Canada and Vancouver?
3. Would you like to do a homestay? Why or why not?
4. If you did a homestay, what would you talk about with your host family?
5. What would you miss about your own home if you did a homestay?

Map of Stanley Park

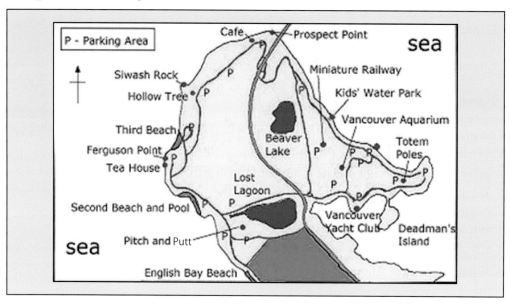

Look at the map of Stanley Park. According to the map, are the following sentences true or false?

1. The café is at the south end of the park.
2. There are fewer than ten parking areas.
3. There are three beaches.
4. The totem poles are in the west of the park.
5. There's an aquarium in the park.

Dialogue: Meeting at the airport

Listen to the conversation and fill in the blanks.

In the arrivals hall.

Mr. Jones Excuse me. Are you Yuta Tanaka?

    Yuta Yes, I am. You must be Mr. Jones. Nice to meet you.

Mr. Jones Hi, nice to meet you. I'm glad I found you. Welcome to Canada. (1)__ _____?

    Yuta Yes, thank you. It was a long flight, but I was able to get a few hours' sleep.

Mr. Jones Can I help you with your bag? Wow, you're traveling light!

    Yuta Actually, my suitcase is missing.

Mr. Jones Oh, no! Have you managed to sort that out?

    Yuta Don't worry. I already filled out a form in the baggage hall. They say they should be able to deliver it tomorrow morning.

Mr. Jones Oh, good. In that case let's go. (*They start walking.*) (2)_____ _____. Oh, by the way, if you feel like doing something this afternoon, I thought we could take a walk in Stanley Park.

    Yuta That would be great. I'd like to get some exercise after sitting on the plane for such a long time.

Mr. Jones OK, I'll take you home and let you rest for a few hours, then we'll head for the park.

    Yuta (3)_____? Could I borrow a T-shirt and some socks? All my clothes are in my suitcase.

Mr. Jones No problem. Our son is about the same size as you, so I'm sure we can find you some things.

    Yuta Thank you very much.

Mr. Jones Here's my car. (4)_____ to get home. Hop in.

Now practice the dialogue with another student.

Dialogue: At the house

Listen to the dialogue and answer the following questions.

1. What does Yuta notice about the front garden?
2. Why should Yuta keep his door closed when he leaves his bedroom?
3. How many switches and dials does the shower have?
4. Why does Yuta need to be careful with the shower?

— 25 —

They drive up to the Jones's house, and get out of the car. Mrs. Jones comes out to meet them.

Mrs. Jones Welcome to our home. Is your suitcase in the trunk?

Yuta Actually, it's missing. They should deliver it tomorrow, so could I borrow a T-shirt and some socks today?

Mrs. Jones Sure, I'll find some for you.

Yuta Thank you. Wow, your house is beautiful! And you have a cherry tree in the garden.

Mrs. Jones Yes, our homestay student last year said that cherry blossom is important in Japan.

Yuta Yes, that's right. It's a symbol of spring, and many people have parties under the cherry trees when they're in blossom.

Mrs. Jones Well, the cherry blossom has already gone this year, I'm sure we'll have a party outside while you're here.

Yuta Sounds great!

Mrs. Jones Come on in. I'll quickly show you around. This is the living room and kitchen area, and here's the bathroom. That door leads to the back garden. Oh, and this is our cat, Muggle. She's quite sweet but she gets everywhere, so I suggest you keep your bedroom door closed when you leave your room. OK, let me show you your bedroom.

They go upstairs.

Mrs. Jones Here's your bedroom, and in here is a small bathroom. It's for your use only, so you can use it at any time.

Yuta That's great. <u>Is it OK if I</u> take a shower now?

Mrs. Jones Please go ahead. Oh, I'll get you those clothes. I'll leave them outside your door.

Yuta Thank you.

Mrs. Jones leaves. Yuta tries the shower but can't turn it on. He goes to the door.

Yuta Oh, Mrs. Jones. Could you show me how the shower works?

Mrs. Jones Oh, I'm sorry. I forgot to tell you about it. It's an electric shower, so you switch it on here. Please switch it off when you finish. There are two dials. This upper one is water pressure. I recommend you always turn it to high pressure. The other dial is for the temperature. This shower is a bit sensitive, and it can get too hot or cold very quickly. I would keep it at about 7.

Yuta Let me just check I understand. This switch is for the electricity ... this controls the water pressure, which I should turn to high ... and this controls the temperature, which I should keep at about 7.

Mrs. Jones Perfect. I'll just get those clothes. See you in a bit.

Yuta Thanks a lot, Mrs. Jones.

Now practice the conversation with another student.

Vocabulary check

Read each definition and write down the correct word.

1. a disc that is turned to select volume, temperature, etc.: d_____
2. an object or sign that represents something else: s_____
3. affected by small changes: s_____
4. on a higher floor: u_____
5. flowers on a tree: b_____
6. advise: s_____

Role play

Read through the dialogues. Then close your books and act out the situations.

A: Yuta Tanaka
B: Mr. Jones, Mrs. Jones

Key expression: *Is it OK if I ...?*

> **Yuta:** Is it OK if I take a shower now?
Mrs. Jones: Please go ahead.

Work with another student. You are in a classroom. Ask permission from your teacher.

Example
A: It's cold in here. Is it OK if I close the window?
B: No problem/Please go ahead. / I'm sorry, but I think we need some fresh air in here.

Student A
1. It's hot in here.
3. My computer's battery is running low.
5. I think I left my bag in the cafeteria.

Student B
2. I have a problem with a contact lens.
4. I'm feeling very tired.
6. I brought the wrong textbook.

Dialogue writing

Work with another student. Use the key expression on page 27 to write a short skit between a professor and a student in a seminar. Use the "notes" pages at the back of the book. Start with the following:

> **Professor:** *Good afternoon. Is everyone here?*
>   **Student:** *Unfortunately, John can't make it. He has a fever this morning.*
> **Professor:** *Oh no! In that case, can you give your presentation today, Keisuke?*
>   **Student:**

Practice the dialogue with your partner.
Close your book and practice the skit from memory.

Discussion

Work with another student. Ask and answer the following questions.

1. If someone came to your hometown, where would you take them sightseeing?
2. What are the main benefits of doing a homestay?
3. What problems do you think people have when they do homestays?
4. If you planned to do a homestay, where would you go?
5. What is your favorite room in your home, and why?
6. What kind of animal would you like to have as a pet, and why?
7. Which do you prefer, baths or showers, and why?

Online research task

Work in a small group. Do an internet search to find out about Vancouver. Choose a famous sightseeing spot that interests you.
  * *Watch a YouTube video about it.*
  * *Use Google Maps and an online encyclopedia to learn more.*
  * *Make notes about three things you learned, and share them with another group. Answer their questions using the internet if necessary.*

> ***Example*** We researched *Stanley Park*. We learned three things: *(1) The park is very big (about 1,001 acres, which is larger than New York's Central Park), (2) there is an aquarium with many sea animals, and (3) there is a 5.5-mile seawall path that is popular for walking, running, and cycling, with nice views of the city and harbor.*

Self-study

Canada

Match the words to the definitions.

1. province___	a) the practice of growing crops and raising animals for food, medicines, and other products
2. ethnically___	b) the business of producing industrial goods such as cars and clothes
3. multicultural___	c) the part of a country's economy that produces raw materials such as oil and food crops
4. immigration___	d) including people from many different cultures
5. manufacturing___	e) relating to a cultural or racial group, often one that is in a minority
6. agriculture___	f) an area that is governed as part of a country
7. primary sector___	g) the act of people from abroad entering a country to live there

Listen to the recording and write the answers.

1. How big is Canada?
2. Who is the head of state?
3. What are Canada's two official languages?
4. What is the population of Canada?
5. What are Canada's two biggest primary sector industries?
6. What share of global oil resources does Canada have?

Dialogue review

Read through the unit and answer the following questions.

1. What plan did Mr. Jones have for the afternoon?
2. Why did Yuta like the idea?
3. What was in the front garden?
4. What was the problem with Muggle?
5. Where did Mrs. Jones say she would leave the clothes?
6. What was the problem with the shower?

Unit 5: Crossing the border

In this unit, you are going to:
- study and practice some breakfast and border-crossing conversations
- practice *"Let me think ..."*
- discuss travel experiences
- research Canada and the USA

Warm up

Work with another student. Ask and answer the following questions.

1. Describe the photographs.
2. What places would you like to visit in the USA, and why?
3. What are the advantages and disadvantages of traveling by bus?
4. Talk about the longest bus trip that you have ever taken.
5. What ID cards do you have, and when do you use them?

Bus schedule

SELECT A DEPARTURE: Saturday, August 23, 20XX
Departure: Vancouver, BC
Arrival: Seattle, WA

Departing	Arriving	Travel Time	Transfers	ADVANCED PURCHASE	WEB ONLY FARE	STANDARD FARE	REFUNDABLE
08:30 AM Sat, 08/23	12:20 AM Sat, 08/23	3H, 50M	0	$38.00	$42.00	$62.00	$105.00
11:15 AM Sat, 08/23	03:55 PM Sat, 08/23	4H, 40M	0	$38.00	$42.00	$62.00	$105.00

SELECT A RETURN: Monday, August 25, 20XX
Departure: Seattle, WA
Arrival: Vancouver, BC

Departing	Arriving	Travel Time	Transfers	ADVANCED PURCHASE	WEB ONLY FARE	STANDARD FARE	REFUNDABLE
02:30 PM Mon 8/25	06:40 PM Mon 8/25	4H, 10M	0	INCLUDED	INCLUDED	INCLUDED	INCLUDED

All schedule times are based on local time zones.

Look at Yuta's search results for the bus schedule, and answer the questions.

1. On what date is Yuta planning to leave Vancouver?
2. How much will Yuta pay if he buys the ticket on the internet?
3. Which bus from Vancouver is better for traveling time?
4. What time will the returning bus from Seattle arrive in Vancouver?

Dialogue: At breakfast

Listen to the conversation and fill in the blanks.

Yuta enters the kitchen.

Yuta Good morning, Mrs. Jones.

Mrs. Jones Oh, good morning, Yuta. Did you sleep well?

Yuta I got a few hours' sleep. Unfortunately, I have jet lag, so I feel a bit groggy.

Mrs. Jones In that case, (1) _____?

Yuta Yes please. That would be great.

Mrs. Jones You must be hungry. Would you like some bacon and eggs?

Yuta Actually, just some toast and cereal please. Mrs. Jones, (2) _____
_____?

Mrs. Jones Sure. What's up?

Yuta I want to visit my friend in Seattle next weekend. Do you know the best way to get there?

Mrs. Jones Oh, if I were you, I'd take the Greyhound bus. It's cheap and you'll get to see some of the scenery on the way down to Seattle. (3)____
_____ on the internet after breakfast.

Yuta Thank you.

Mrs. Jones Also, you'll need to fill out some immigration forms on the internet. Otherwise, you'll get stuck at the border.

Yuta Oh, do I have to get a visa?

Mrs. Jones I doubt it. I think Japanese passport holders don't need to get one, but we can check. Here's your coffee. (4)_____
_____. Later, I'll also show you where everything else is in the kitchen.

Yuta Thank you very much.

Now practice the conversation with another student.

Dialogue: At the border

1. What is Yuta's friend doing in the USA?
2. How long is Yuta going to stay in the USA?
3. Where is Yuta's plane ticket?
4. Which place did Yuta visit in the USA on a previous trip?

Yuta approaches the immigration officer and hands him his passport.

Officer Why are you visiting the States?

  Yuta I'm going to do some sightseeing with a friend.

Officer Is your friend on the bus?

  Yuta No, I'm going to meet him in Seattle.

Officer Where do you know him from?

  Yuta We're at university together in Japan.

Officer And what's he doing in the United States?

  Yuta He's doing a homestay and a short course. We're both studying to be English teachers.

Officer So, what have you been doing in Canada?

  Yuta I'm also doing a homestay to improve my English.

Officer Where will you be staying in the States?

  Yuta With my friend's homestay family. Here's the address: The Thomsens, 20 Ocean Drive, Seattle.

Yuta passes him his notebook.

Officer OK. How long will you be in the States?

  Yuta Just for a few days. Then, I'll go back to Vancouver.

Officer Do you have a round trip ticket to Canada?

  Yuta Yes, here it is.

Officer And please show me your plane ticket back to Japan.

  Yuta Ah, that's with my homestay family in Vancouver. I left it with them for safety.

Officer What's their address?

  Yuta Here it is: Mr. and Mrs. Jones, 21 Cedar Avenue, Vancouver.

Officer Do you have something to verify that you're returning to Japan?

  Yuta <u>Let me think</u> ... I'm a university student. Here's my university card, and my semester starts in October. Oh, wait a minute. I don't have my ticket, but this is the receipt for it that I got from my travel agent.

Yuta shows the officer his plane ticket receipt.

Officer Thank you. Have you been in the United States before?

  Yuta Yes, I went to Hawaii when I was a high school student.

Officer That's all.

  Yuta Thank you.

Now practice the conversation with another student.

Vocabulary check

Read each definition and write down the correct word.

1. to make something better: i_____
2. another name for the USA: the S_____
3. a situation of no risk or danger: s_____
4. to confirm or prove: v_____
5. a period of teaching months at a university: s_____
6. a piece of paper that shows something has been paid for: r_____

Role play

Read through the dialogues. Then close your books and act out the situations.

A: Yuta Tanaka
B: Mrs. Jones, immigration officer

Key expression: *Let me think ...*

Officer: Do you have something to verify that you're returning to Japan?

   Yuta: Let me think ... I'm a university student. Here's my university card, and my semester starts in October. Oh, wait a minute. I don't have my ticket, but this is the receipt for it that I got from my travel agent.

Work with another student. Listen to the question and reply.

Example
A: How much green tea do you drink in a week?
B: Let me think ... I drink two cups every morning at breakfast, and from Monday to Friday I have a cup of green tea in the afternoon as well, so that's fourteen plus five – I drink nineteen cups of green tea a week. Wow!

Student A

1. How much time do you spend on your smartphone in a day?
3. How much time do you spend traveling to and from university in a week?
5. How many bowls of rice do you eat in a week?

Student B

2. How many liters of liquid do you drink in a day?
4. How much time do you spend on homework in a week?
6. How many hours do you sleep in a week?

Dialogue writing

Work with another student. Imagine that two students are planning to go on a diet. They are thinking about their eating habits, and how to change them. Use the key expression on page 33 to write the dialogue. Use the "notes" pages at the back of the book. Start with the following:

> **Peter:** *Let's plan how we're going to lose weight. How should we start?*
>
> **Makiko:** *Well, we need to think about what we eat, and then decide how we can change our eating habits. How much chcolate … ?*
>
> **Peter:**

Practice the dialogue with your partner.
Close your book and practice the skit from memory.

Discussion

Work with another student. Ask and answer the following questions.

1. What do you usually eat for breakfast?
2. Describe a traditional Japanese breakfast.
3. What advice do you have for someone who can't get to sleep easily?
4. Which parts of Japan have the most beautiful scenery?
5. What do you carry in your wallet when you go on a trip?
6. Do you like credit cards? Why or why not?

Online research task

Work in a small group. Do an internet search to find out about the area near the Canada-US border. Choose a famous sightseeing spot that interests you.

- *Watch a YouTube video about it.*
- *Use Google Maps and an online encyclopedia to learn more.*
- *Make notes about three things you learned, and share them with another group. Answer their questions using the internet if necessary.*

> **Example** We researched *Niagara Falls. It's a group of three huge waterfalls on the Canada-US border.* Three things we learned are: *(1) It generates hydroelectric power, (2) visitors can take a boat tour to get close to the falls, and (3) it's considered one of the natural wonders of the world.*

Self-study
The USA and the American Revolution

Match the words to the definitions.

1. federation___	a) having the function of making laws
	b) relating to courts of law and judges
2. constitution___	c) a group of states joined together to form a larger state and government
3. democracy___	d) a country or area controlled politically by a more powerful country
4. legislative___	e) a set of political principles by which a country is governed
5. executive___	f) relating to decision-making and administration in public affairs
6. judicial___	g) government by the people, usually through elected representatives
7. colony___	

Listen to the recording and write the answers.
1. What is the population of the USA?
2. How many branches of the federal government are there?
3. Where were the 13 British colonies in North America located?
4. When did the American Revolutionary War start?
5. What three rights were stated at the beginning of the Declaration of Independence?
6. What is July 4th called?

Dialogue review

Read through the unit and answer the following questions.
1. What did Yuta want for breakfast?
2. Where did Yuta want to go on the weekend?
3. Why was Yuta's friend in Seattle?
4. Where was Yuta going to stay in Seattle?
5. Where was Yuta's plane ticket?
6. What part of the USA had Yuta previously visited?

Unit 6: Visiting a museum

In this unit, you are going to:

- study and practice some conversations at a museum
- practice *"Excuse me. Are you OK?"*
- discuss local attractions such as museums
- research Seattle and aviation in the USA

Warm up

Work with another student. Ask and answer the following questions.

1. Describe the photographs.
2. What do you know about the USA and Seattle?
3. When was the last time you went to a museum? What did you see?
4. Have you ever lost something? What did you do?

Extract from Wings Café Menu

Beverages		Hours
Orange or Apple Juice	$3.00	**Monday – Sunday**
Bottled Water	$3.00	**10:00 am – 5:00 pm**
Milk (Regular or Chocolate Milk)	$2.00	
Regular or Decaf Coffee & Tea	$3.00	**First Thursday of the Month**
Domestic Beer	$6.00	**10:00 am – 9:00 pm**
Micro Brews & Imported Beer	$7.00	
		9404 East Marginal Way S.
Fountain Beverages	$3.50	**Seattle, WA 98108**
Coke, Diet Coke, Sprite, Root Beer,		
Lemonade & Iced Tea (One free refill)		

All prices exclude 9.5% Sales Tax

Look at the extract from the menu and answer the following questions.
1. What is the cheapest drink?
2. What is the advantage of buying one of the "fountain beverages"?
3. What do all the prices *not* include?
4. On what day does the café stay open until 9:00 p.m.?

Dialogue: **At the museum café**

Listen to the conversation and fill in the blanks.

Yuta goes up to the counter.
        Yuta A regular coffee, please.
Café employee (1)_____?
        Yuta Yes, I'll have one of those bagels.
The café employee gives Yuta a tray with the coffee and bagel. Yuta hands over a $10 bill.
Café employee Here's your receipt and change.
        Yuta Thank you.
The restaurant is very crowded. There are no empty tables. Yuta goes up to a table which has only one customer.
        Yuta Excuse me. It's very crowded. (2)_____
_____?
Customer Sure. Go ahead.
        Yuta Thanks.
Customer Have you been round the museum?
        Yuta Not yet. (3)_____. How about you?
Customer Yeah. (4)_____. My kids have gone
           shopping in the museum store.
        Yuta Is there anything you recommend in the museum?
Customer Yeah. We had a lot of fun on a flight simulator.
        Yuta What's that?
Customer Well, you pretend to fly a plane using a computer program in a
           kind of box that looks like an airplane cockpit.
        Yuta Oh, I'll give it a try. (5)_____.
Customer You're welcome. I'd better go find my kids before they try to
           buy the whole store! Enjoy the museum. See you.
        Yuta See you.

Dialogue: **At the flight simulators**

Listen to the dialogue and answer the following questions.
1. What does Yuta lose?
2. Where does the museum attendant look first for the lost item?
3. What does the museum attendant ask his colleague Jan to do?
4. How does Yuta identify his lost property?

Yuta comes out of the flight simulator looking pale and worried. A museum attendant walks up to him.

Attendant Excuse me, sir. Are you OK?

    Yuta Not really. I've lost my camera.

Attendant Did you have it when you came into the museum?

    Yuta Yes, I think so.

Attendant And what places have you been to in the museum?

    Yuta Only this simulator.

Attendant OK, let me just check inside the simulator. Sometimes cameras, wallets or keys fall down the side of the seats or onto the floor.

The attendant checks inside the simulator.

Attendant It's not there. Is there anywhere else you've been in the museum? The restrooms, the store ...

    Yuta The coffee shop!

Attendant Wing's Café?

    Yuta Yes, I went there before I got my museum ticket.

Attendant OK, let's check there. If we can't find it, we'll go to the lost property office. Just one moment. I need to talk to my colleague.

The attendant turns to a colleague.

Attendant Jan, could you look after the simulator for ten minutes? I have to help this gentleman look for his camera.

    Jan Sure.

They walk to Wings Café and enter the seating area.

Attendant Where were you sitting?

    Yuta At that table over there.

Attendant Do you see the camera?

    Yuta No, I don't.

Attendant Let me ask the café staff.

The attendant goes over to the counter of the café and talks to the café staff. He comes back with two cameras.

Attendant Is one of these yours?

    Yuta Yes, that looks like it. Let me check the memory. Yes, this is my camera. Here's a photo of my homestay family and their cat. Thank you so much for your help.

Attendant No problem. They were going to take the cameras to the lost property office at the end of the morning shift. This kind of thing happens a lot.

    Yuta Thank you very much. I thought I'd lost all the photos of my trip.

Attendant You're welcome. Enjoy the rest of the museum.

Now practice the conversation with another student.

Vocabulary check

Read each definition and write down the correct word.

1. a room with toilets in a public place: r_____
2. personal objects that have been left by accident: l_____ p_____
3. a very short period of time: m_____
4. one of a group of people who work together: c_____
5. data storage space in a computer: m_____
6. a scheduled time period in which people work: sh_____

Role play

Read through the dialogues. Then close your books and act out the situations.

A: Yuta Tanaka, Jan
B: café employee, customer, museum attendant

Key expression: *Excuse me. Are you OK?*

Attendant: Excuse me, sir. Are you OK?
     Yuta: Not really. I've lost my camera.

Work with another student. Offer help, listen to the problem, and give advice.

Example

A: Excuse me. Are you OK?
B: No, I can't find my bag!
A: Where did you last have it?
B: I had it in my morning class.
A: OK, let's go and check the classroom.

Student A

1. I've lost my phone!
3. I'm looking for a bus stop.
5. Someone's just run off with my wallet!

Student B

2. I'm feeling very weak.
4. I'm looking for the nearest restroom
6. I've lost my umbrella!

Dialogue writing

Work with another student. Two friends, Seiji and Maria, are in a restaurant when Seiji realizes he has lost his wallet. Use the key expression on page 39 to prepare a short skit between the two friends. Use the "notes" pages at the back of the book. Start with the following:

> **Maria:** *This food is really good. Seiji, you look very pale! ...*
>   **Seiji:**
> **Maria:**

Practice the dialogue with your partner.
Close your book and practice the skit from memory.

Discussion

Work with another student. Ask and answer the following questions.

1. What museums are there in or near your hometown?
2. What kinds of places do you like to visit when you are traveling?
3. What kind of tourist attraction (park, museum, etc.) would you like to have in your local area, and why?
4. If you lost your wallet while you were traveling, what would you do?
5. What are the good points and bad points of computer/video games?
6. Which part of the USA would you most like to visit, and why?

Online research task

Work in a small group. Do an internet search to find out about Seattle. Choose a famous sightseeing spot that interests you.
- *Watch a YouTube video about it.*
- *Use Google Maps and an online encyclopedia to learn more.*
- *Make notes about three things you learned, and share them with another group. Answer their questions using the internet if necessary.*

> **Example** We researched *the Space Needle. It's a 184-meter observation tower built for the 1962 World's Fair.* We learned three things: *(1) Visitors can ride an elevator to the observation deck, (2) the tower offers panoramic views of the city, and (3) the top of the tower has a rotating restaurant.*

Self-study
Aviation in the USA

Match the words to the definitions.

1. aviation___	a) relating to products and services for sale to the general public
2. adjustment___	b) someone who repairs or maintains engines
3. stability___	c) the amount that can be contained in something
4. mechanic___	d) a situation in which something is not likely to move or change
5. fabric___	e) a kind of evergreen tree with needle-like leaves
6. commercial___	f) the activity of designing, flying, building, or maintaining airplanes
7. capacity___	g) cloth or material for covering furniture or making clothes
8. spruce___	h) a small change made to improve something

Listen to the recording and write answers to the following questions.

1. What kind of business did the Wright brothers run?
2. Who built the engine for Flyer 1?
3. When did the brothers first fly the airplane (Flyer 1)?
4. Why did William E. Boeing base his company in Seattle?
5. When did the Boeing 747s go into service?
6. What was the effect of the 747s on ticket prices?

S 31

Dialogue review

Read through the unit and answer the following questions.

1. What did Yuta buy at the museum café?
2. Why were the customer's children not at the table in the café?
3. What was the name of the coffee shop?
4. Who was Jan?
5. How many cameras did the museum attendant show Yuta?
6. When were the café staff going to take the cameras to the lost property office?

Review Section of Units 1–6

1. *Look at units 1 to 6 and choose three units. What problem did Yuta have in the units you have chosen?*

Unit (　　　) :＿＿＿＿＿＿＿＿＿＿＿＿＿＿＿＿＿＿＿＿＿＿＿

＿＿＿＿＿＿＿＿＿＿＿＿＿＿＿＿＿＿＿＿＿＿＿＿＿＿＿＿＿＿＿＿

Unit (　　　) :＿＿＿＿＿＿＿＿＿＿＿＿＿＿＿＿＿＿＿＿＿＿＿

＿＿＿＿＿＿＿＿＿＿＿＿＿＿＿＿＿＿＿＿＿＿＿＿＿＿＿＿＿＿＿＿

Unit (　　　) :＿＿＿＿＿＿＿＿＿＿＿＿＿＿＿＿＿＿＿＿＿＿＿

＿＿＿＿＿＿＿＿＿＿＿＿＿＿＿＿＿＿＿＿＿＿＿＿＿＿＿＿＿＿＿＿

2. *How did he solve the problems in those three units?*

Unit (　　　) :＿＿＿＿＿＿＿＿＿＿＿＿＿＿＿＿＿＿＿＿＿＿＿

＿＿＿＿＿＿＿＿＿＿＿＿＿＿＿＿＿＿＿＿＿＿＿＿＿＿＿＿＿＿＿＿

Unit (　　　) :＿＿＿＿＿＿＿＿＿＿＿＿＿＿＿＿＿＿＿＿＿＿＿

＿＿＿＿＿＿＿＿＿＿＿＿＿＿＿＿＿＿＿＿＿＿＿＿＿＿＿＿＿＿＿＿

Unit (　　　) :＿＿＿＿＿＿＿＿＿＿＿＿＿＿＿＿＿＿＿＿＿＿＿

＿＿＿＿＿＿＿＿＿＿＿＿＿＿＿＿＿＿＿＿＿＿＿＿＿＿＿＿＿＿＿＿

3. *With a partner, choose one unit. Read the second dialogue aloud by yourself. Then practice the conversation with your partner.*

4. *Close your books and role-play the conversation.*

5. *Choose one of Yuta's journeys below and write a summary of it with a title. Use the "notes" pages at the back of the book for the summary.*

  a. Singapore, London, and Edinburgh

  b. Vancouver and Seattle

Read your partner's summary and write some comments and questions.

6. *Choose one of Yuta's experiences from Units 1 to 6 in the book and present (1) a summary of it to the class with a focus on the problem and how he solved it along with (2) your personal reflection on the topic. Prepare visuals using PowerPoint or other software for your presentation. Use the past tense when writing your script. Use your own words to present the summary.*

Example: *(1) I am going to talk about Yuta's trip from Singapore to London. He traveled by plane and first he had to present his passport and e-ticket at the check-in desk ...*
(2) Now, let me share my thoughts. I think traveling alone by plane is a good opportunity to start a conversation and make some friends. Yuta was very lucky to sit next to a passenger who could recommend places to him in London ...

Listen to the presentations and write questions you want to ask.

Unit 7: One-day tour

Warm up

Work with another student. Ask and answer the following questions.

1. Describe the photographs.
2. What do you know about India?
3. What do you like or dislike about guided tours, and why?
4. What's the longest journey that you have ever made?

Tour itinerary: Taj Mahal tour

0630 – 1100 hours
Drive to Agra through the Indian countryside. (Delhi – Agra 230 km, 4 hours 30 min. approx.)

1100 – 1230 hours
On arrival, visit the Taj Mahal, built in 1652 by Emperor Shah Jahan. This building is a fine example of the mixture of many architectural styles.

1300 – 1400 hours
Have lunch (buffet) at the Hotel Trident.

1400 – 1500 hours
Visit the Agra Fort, built in red sandstone, with its magnificent palaces.

1500 – 1530 hours
Visit a marble factory.

1600 – 1630 hours
Make a brief visit to Sikandra, the tomb of the Mughal Emperor Akbar.

1630 – 1930 hours
Return to Delhi.

Look at the website information and answer the following questions.

1. How far is it from Delhi to Agra?
2. What kind of lunch will the passengers eat?
3. What will they do from 2:00 p.m. to 3:00 p.m.?
4. What is "Sikandra"?
5. What time will they reach Delhi in the evening?

Dialogue: **At the hotel reception desk, 6:20 a.m.**

Listen to the conversation and fill in the blanks.

Hana approaches the receptionist.
Receptionist Good morning, madam.
Hana Good morning. (1)_____ to Agra and I've been instructed to wait at reception.
Receptionist <u>Could you tell me</u> the name of the tour company?
Hana Yes, it's Raja Tours.
Receptionist Ah, yes. The tour guide will come here to pick up passengers from this hotel. He usually comes a few minutes early. (2)_____, I'll let him know when he arrives.
Hana takes a seat and a few minutes later a man comes over.
Tour Guide Good morning. My name is Raj Patel from Raja Tours. (3)_____?
Hana Yes, I am.
Tour Guide Do you have the tour ticket?
Hana passes him the ticket.
Tour Guide Thank you. I have one more passenger to pick up from this hotel, so (4)_____ until he arrives.
The receptionist signals the tour guide. A sleepy young man is standing by the reception desk.
Tour Guide That must be the other passenger. (5)_____.

Now practice the conversation with another student.

Dialogue: **On the tour bus**

Listen to the dialogue and answer the following questions.

1. How many rest stops will the bus make on the way to Agra?
2. What problem does the passenger have?
3. Who is Hana going to meet in Delhi?
4. What does Mike have to do next year?

There are 10 passengers, the tour guide, and the driver.

Tour Guide Good morning. My name is Raj Patel, and I am your tour guide today. Welcome to Raja Tours. Today we are going to do the Agra tour. We'll visit two very famous sites: the Taj Mahal and the Agra Fort. The journey will take about four and a half hours, so we will take rest stops every 90 minutes. I will point out sites of interest while we are traveling.

Passenger Excuse me. Do you have anything to drink on the bus?

Tour Guide I'm afraid not, but you can pick up soft drinks at each stop on the way.

Hana Are you OK?

Passenger Not really. I didn't have time for breakfast this morning, and I have a slight headache.

Hana Have you had anything to drink this morning?

Passenger No, I didn't have time.

Hana You're probably dehydrated. I have a spare bottle of water if you want it.

She passes him the water.

Passenger Thank you. That's very kind of you. I'll buy a fresh bottle at the next stop. You seem very well prepared.

Hana Well, I'm a medical student, so I tend to carry water and a small medicine bag with me while I'm traveling.

Passenger In that case, do you have an aspirin by any chance?

Hana I do. Just give me a moment to find one.

She hands him an aspirin.

Passenger You're a star! My name's Mike, by the way. I'm a student at Exeter University.

Hana My name's Hana. I'm at Hiroshima University.

Passenger So Hana, are you on holiday?

Hana Partly. I'm also visiting some medical schools in Delhi to meet some students and find out about healthcare here in India.

Passenger Wow, that's great! I'm here for the sights and sounds. Next year, I have to take my final exams and I have to find a job, so this is one of my last chances to do a big tour. How long have you been in Delhi? ...

Now practice the conversation with another student.

Vocabulary check

Read each definition and write down the correct word.

1. a soft browny-red or brown type of stone: s_____
2. very good, deserving admiration: m_____
3. to collect or obtain: p_____ u_____
4. likely to be the case: p_____
5. physically needing water: d_____
6. important last set of tests at university: f_____ e_____

Role play

Read through the dialogues. Then close your books and act out the situations.

A: Hana Suzuki
B: receptionist, tour guide, passenger

Key expression: *Could you tell me ...?*

Receptionist: Could you tell me the name of the tour company?
Hana: Yes, it's Raja Tours.

Work with another student. Listen to the requests and give answers.

Example

A: Excuse me. Could you tell me the name of this building?
B: Yes, it's Building K.

Student A

1. ... the time?
3. ... where I can buy a magazine?
5. ... the name of your faculty or department?

Student B

2. ... the name of your English teacher?
4. ... where I can get some coffee near here?
6. ... what time we finish this class?

Dialogue writing

Work with another student. Tom is in a travel agent's office in Japan and wants to take a one-day tour of the local area. Use the key expression on page 47 to prepare a short skit between Tom and the travel agent. Use the "notes" pages at the back of the book. Start with the following:

> **Tom:** *Good morning.*
> **Travel agent:** *Good morning, sir. How can I help you?*
> **Tom:**

Practice the dialogue with your partner.
Close your book and practice the skit from memory.

Discussion

T 03

Work with another student. Ask and answer the following questions.

1. What do you usually carry with you while you are traveling?
2. If you have a headache, what do you usually do?
3. Would you like to take the Taj Mahal tour on page 44? Why or why not?
4. Where is the warmest place you have ever visited?
5. Which Indian dishes or drinks have you tried?
6. If you went to India, what would you do there?

Online research task

Work in a small group. Do an internet search to find out more about India. Choose a sightseeing spot that interests you.
- *Watch a YouTube video about it.*
- *Use Google Maps and an online encyclopedia to learn more.*
- *Make notes about the place, including three things you learned, and share them with another group. Answer their questions using the internet if necessary.*

> ***Example*** We researched *Mumbai. It's the wealthiest city in India and a global financial hub.* We learned three things: *(1) A top attraction is Bollywood (India's largest film industry), (2) visitors can enjoy the many different kinds of street food available in the city, and (3) Mumbai is known as a paradise for shopaholics.*

Self-study
India, spices, cotton, and Gandhi

Match the words to the definitions.

1. producer___	a) to bring goods and services into a country from abroad
2. gradually___	b) a planned set of political or military actions with a particular aim
3. reject___	c) social position or rank
4. campaign___	d) treating people differently because of factors such as skin color or sexuality
5. discrimination___	e) a country or group that provides goods
6. import___	f) slowly over a period of time
7. status___	g) to refuse to accept or use something

Listen to the recording and write the answers to the following questions.
1. What does 26% of India's GDP come from?
2. In relation to trade, what was the most important spice in India?
3. What did Vasco de Gama do?
4. In the twentieth century, when did India become an independent republic?
5. In 1930, what did Gandhi campaign against?
6. What does "Mahatma" mean?

S 32

Dialogue review

Read through the unit and answer the following questions.
1. What time did Hana approach the reception desk?
2. What was the name of the tour company?
3. What are the two very famous sights on the tour?
4. What did Hana give Mike?
5. Where was Mike studying?
6. What was Hana doing in Delhi?

Unit 8: At a company office

In this unit, you are going to:
- study and practice some office conversations
- practice *"Would you like ...?"*
- discuss Thailand and working abroad
- research Bangkok and Thailand

Warm up

Work with another student. Ask and answer the following questions.

1. Describe the photographs.
2. What do you know about Thailand?
3. Would you like to work abroad?
4. What do you know about the vehicle in the picture on the right?

Car manufacturing in Thailand

Thailand calls itself the "Detroit of South-East Asia" after the famous American car-making city. Japanese automobile makers have invested heavily in the country, with three of the biggest being Toyota, Honda, and Isuzu. For example, in 2022, Honda employed 275,000 people in Thailand. In addition, there are many companies that make car parts, supplying them to nearby car plants as well as exporting them.

Electric vehicles (EVs) are expected to become an important market in the future, and the Thai government has announced a plan for 30 percent of automobile production to be EVs by 2030. In Thailand, Toyota is going to produce its first electric pickup truck for emerging markets, and Honda plans to produce all-electric SUVs (sports utility vehicles). In addition to Japanese automobile makers, Chinese companies such as BYD and Taiwan's Foxconn also have plans to produce EVs in the country.

Read the magazine article and answer the following questions.

1. What does Thailand call itself?
2. How many people did Honda employ in 2022?
3. What plan has the Thai government announced?
4. What does SUV stand for?
5. What other companies have plans to produce electric vehicles in Thailand?

Dialogue: **At the company office**

S 16
T 04

Listen to the conversation and fill in the blanks.

Hana goes up to the reception desk.

      Hana Good afternoon. My name's Hana Suzuki. I'm here to meet Daigo Suzuki.

Receptionist One moment, please. (*The receptionist picks up the phone and talks to someone in Thai.*) (1)_____ to meet you. Please take a seat.

Hana sits down. After a few minutes a smartly dressed person walks up to her.

    Assistant Ms. Suzuki? I'm Rattana, Mr. Suzuki's assistant. Unfortunately, your brother had to go to an emergency meeting in Chiang Mai this morning. (2)_____ until he returns.

      Hana Did he say when he was coming back?

    Assistant Yes – sometime tomorrow afternoon. He left his apartment keys and a note for you. What we'll do now is go to a meeting room and (3)_____.

      Hana Thank you.

They reach the meeting room.

    Assistant You must be tired. <u>Would you like</u> something to drink? Coffee, tea, Coca Cola?

      Hana A cup of coffee would be great.

    Assistant A coffee. Milk? Sugar?

      Hana (4)_____.

    Assistant Please take a seat, and (5)_____with the coffee.

      Hana Thank you.

Now practice the conversation with another student.

Dialogue: **In the meeting room**

S 17
T 05

Listen to the dialogue and answer the following questions.

1. How long was the flight from Delhi?
2. How long does it take to walk to the apartment?
3. What has Daigo promised to do on Sunday?
4. What are Hana and the assistant going to do tomorrow?

The assistant enters with two cups of coffee.

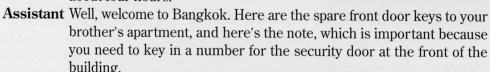

Assistant One black coffee.

Hana Thank you.

Assistant Did you have a good journey?

Hana Yes, I flew from Delhi, so it only took about four hours.

Assistant Well, welcome to Bangkok. Here are the spare front door keys to your brother's apartment, and here's the note, which is important because you need to key in a number for the security door at the front of the building.

Hana I'm sorry, I don't understand. I need a key for the security door?

Assistant No, there's a four-digit number for the security door. He's written it in the note I just gave you, along with the address.

Hana Oh, I see – a four-number code. (*She quickly scans the note.*) Yes, I see it. Is the apartment far from here?

Assistant Actually, it's quite close. Your brother usually walks here in about twenty minutes. I'll take you over there shortly, but as you have a suitcase and it's very hot and humid today, I've organized a taxi.

Hana Thank you.

Assistant He told me that there's plenty of fresh food and drink in the fridge. He also asked me to show you some of the sights of Bangkok tomorrow. Would you like to see the Grand Palace?

Hana That would be great, if it's not too much trouble.

Assistant It's no problem. The office is closed at the weekend, and I have a free day. Besides, your brother has promised to take us to the best restaurant in Bangkok on Sunday.

Hana Well, I look forward to it!

Assistant I have his home number, so I'll ring you tomorrow around 9:30 and pick you up around 9:45. We can visit the Grand Palace before lunch. Depending on how you're feeling, I can also take you on a river tour.

Hana Sounds wonderful! If there are any problems, how can I contact you?

Assistant Here's my business card. Is there anything else you need?

Hana No, that's fine.

Assistant I'll leave you here for a few minutes to relax and finish your coffee. I'll come and get you when the taxi arrives.

Hana Thank you so much.

Now practice the conversation with another student.

Vocabulary check

Read each definition and write down the correct word.

1. a company that makes physical products: m_____
2. a factory containing machines for production: p_____
3. goods that are sent abroad for sale: e_____
4. relating to a damp feeling in the air: h_____
5. in addition to/also: b_____
6. to be decided based on something in the future: d_____

Role play

Read through the dialogues. Then close your books and act out the situations.

A: Hana Suzuki
B: receptionist, assistant

Key expression: *Would you like ...?*

Assistant: He also asked me to show you some of the sights of Bangkok tomorrow. Would you like to see the Grand Palace?

Hana: That would be great, if you're sure it's not too much trouble.

Work with another student. Listen to the questions and give replies.

Example
A: Would you like a cup of coffee?
B: Yes, please. / No, thank you. I'm fine.

A: Would you like to see my vacation photos?
B: Sure. / I'm afraid I'm in a hurry.

Student A
1. ... some help with your bags?
3. ... to go out for a meal?
5. ... to see a movie?

Student B
2. ... to go hiking on the weekend?
4. ... to borrow my textbook?
6. ... a cup of tea?

Dialogue writing

Work with another student. Keisuke meets Dan at lunch and finds out he is moving to a new apartment. Use the key expression on page 53 to prepare a short skit in which Keisuke offers to help. Use the "notes" pages at the back of the book. Start with the following:

> **Dan:** *Hi Keisuke. How's it going?*
>
> **Keisuke:** *Fine, thanks. How are things with you?*
>
> **Dan:** *Actually, I'm moving to a new apartment soon, so I've been really busy.*
>
> **Keisuke:**

Practice the dialogue with your partner.
Close your books and practice the skit from memory.

Discussion

Work with another student. Ask and answer the following questions.

1. What do you know about Bangkok?
2. When you eat out, what do you like to eat?
3. What do you know about Thai food? Would you like to try it?
4. What are the good points and bad points about working abroad?
5. What kind of organization or company would you like to work for in the future?
6. If you could work anywhere abroad for six months, where would you choose to go, and why?

Online research task

Work in a small group. Do an internet search to find out more about Bangkok. Choose a famous sightseeing spot that interests you.
- *Watch a YouTube video about it.*
- *Use Google Maps and an online encyclopedia to learn more.*
- *Make notes about three things you learned, and share them with another group. Answer their questions using the internet if necessary.*

> **Example** We researched *the Emerald Buddha. It's a figure of the Buddha in meditation.* We learned three things: *(1) It is located in the grounds of the Grand Palace, (2) it is 66 cm tall, and (3) the figure is made of jasper (a precious green stone).*

Self-study
Thailand and Bangkok

Match the words to the definitions.

1. rapid___	a) a part that combines with other parts to make something bigger
2. appliance___	b) relating to a particular area or part of the world
3. component___	c) the main offices of an organization
4. vehicle___	d) a large company or group of companies
5. regional___	e) fast or quick
6. headquarters___	f) a machine or device that is used in a house, e.g., a fridge
7. corporation___	g) a machine, usually with wheels, for transporting people, such as a car or a bus

Listen to the recording and write the answers.

S 33

1. How many countries have land borders with Thailand?
2. What is the population of Thailand?
3. What are some of Thailand's major manufacturing industries?
4. What percentage of Thailand's labor force works in agriculture?
5. Which is the most important crop in the country?
6. What do many multinational corporations have in Bangkok?

Dialogue review

Read through the unit and answer the following questions.

1. Why wasn't Daigo at the company office?
2. What did Daigo leave for Hana?
3. What did Hana need for the security door of Daigo's apartment building?
4. What drink did the assistant bring Hana?
5. How were Hana and the assistant going to get to Daigo's apartment?
6. Where had Daigo promised to take Hana and the assistant on Sunday?

Unit 9: Dealing with illness

> **In this unit, you are going to:**
> - study and practice some hotel and medical conversations
> - practice *"May I ...?"*
> - discuss China and health
> - research Shanghai and China

Warm up

Work with another student. Ask and answer the following questions.

1. Describe the photographs.
2. What do you know about China?
3. What do you want to find out about Shanghai?
4. How can you avoid illness while traveling?

Hana's room reservation

Room: SINGLE	
Adults: 1	
Children: 0	
DATE	**PRICE PER NIGHT (CNY*)**
20 Sep 20XX	¥550
21 Sep 20XX	¥550
22 Sep 20XX	¥550
23 Sep 20XX	¥550
Room subtotal	¥2,200
Service charge 15% per room per stay	¥330
Total for stay	¥2,530

If you wish to cancel, please do so 1 day prior to arrival to avoid cancellation penalties. At check in, the front desk will verify your check-out date.

OPTIONAL SERVICES FOR AN ADDITIONAL CHARGE (CNY)
- Parking charges: ¥160 per 24 hours
- In-Room Wi-Fi: ¥160 per 24 hours
- Public Wi-Fi: Complimentary

*CNY = Chinese yuan

1. What is the room rate for one night?
2. How many nights is Hana going to stay?
3. How much does it cost to use the public Wi-Fi?
4. When is the last date that Hana can cancel the booking without penalty charges?
5. What will the front desk verify when Hana checks in?

Dialogue: **At the hotel reception desk**

Listen to the conversation and fill in the blanks.

Hana goes up to the receptionist.

Hana Good evening. I have a reservation.

Receptionist Good evening, madam. May I have your name please?

Hana It's Hana Suzuki.

Receptionist One moment. (*He checks the computer.*) (1)_____ _____, checking out on the 24th of September. Non-smoking.

Hana Yes, that's right. (2)_____?

Receptionist Yes, that's correct.

Hana I'd also like to use the internet in my room.

Receptionist One moment. I have to give you an access code. (3)_____ _____. When you log on, you have to input the code.

Hana And what time is breakfast tomorrow?

Receptionist It starts at 7:00 and finishes at 10:00. (4)_____ _____? (*Hana quickly completes the form.*) Here's your room key. It's room 303. The elevator is over there. Do you need assistance with your bag?

Hana No, thank you. I'll be fine. By the way, (5)_____ _____?

Receptionist No, it closed at 10:00. However, you can order food from the room service menu in your room.

Hana Thank you.

Now practice the conversation with another student.

Dialogue: **A telephone call**

Listen to the dialogue and answer the following questions.

1. What are Hana's symptoms?
2. How long does the illness usually last?
3. What should Hana avoid?
4. What does Hana order from room service?

The telephone rings in Hana's room.

Hana Hello?

Dr. Chang Good morning. Is that Hana Suzuki?

Hana Yes, speaking.

Dr. Chang Hana, this is Dr. Chang. Welcome to Shanghai. Did you have a good flight?

Hana Yes, thank you, but unfortunately I'm sick.

Dr. Chang Oh no! What seems to be the problem?

Hana Well, I had a slight stomachache when I reached the hotel late last night, but I managed to eat some food. Then I started to feel really sick in the middle of the night, and I threw up several times. I also have diarrhea.

Dr. Chang Do you have any other symptoms?

Hana Yes, I have a headache and a slight fever.

Dr. Chang I think you may have caught a norovirus. There's a lot of it in Shanghai at the moment.

Hana What do you think I should do?

Dr. Chang The virus seems to last about 24 hours, so you should stay in bed and see how you feel tomorrow. I'll give you a call around midday to see how you are. I'll rearrange some of the meetings for later in the week. Do you have my number?

Hana Yes, I have it on my computer. You can also contact me by email.

Dr. Chang If you feel a lot worse, give me a call. Make sure you don't dehydrate. Drink plenty of water, and avoid sugar or milk.

Hana OK. I'll do that.

Dr. Chang I hope you feel better soon.

Hana Thank you. Talk to you tomorrow.

Dr. Chang Bye.

Hana puts down the phone, then dials room service.

Room service Room service.

Hana I'd like to order three liters of mineral water.

Room service Could you repeat that?

Hana Yes, three large bottles of mineral water, please.

Room service Er ... anything else?

Hana No, that's fine.

Room service We'll bring them up shortly.

Hana Thank you.

Now practice the conversation with another student.

Vocabulary check

Read each definition and write down the correct word.

1. before: p_____ t_____
2. help: a_____
3. to vomit (be sick): th_____ u_____
4. changes you feel in your body due to a medical problem: s_____
5. to change the order, position, or time of something: r_____
6. to keep away from: a_____

Role play

Read through the dialogues. Then close your books and act out the situations.

A: Hana Suzuki
B: receptionist, Dr. Chang, room service

Key expression: *May I ...?*

Receptionist: Good evening, madam. May I have your name, please?
        Hana: It's Hana Suzuki.

Work with another student. Listen to the requests and accept or reject them.

Example
A: May I have a cup of coffee?
B: Sure, I'll just get you one. / I'm afraid I don't have any coffee.

Student A
1. ... (turn on) the air-conditioning?
3. ... (have) the name of your university or organization?
5. ... (borrow) a pen?

Student B
2. ... (have) something to eat?
4. ... (leave) the class early?
6. ... (use) your smartphone?

Dialogue writing

Work with another student. Jim has found an envelope containing money on the street. He has taken it to a police station. Use the key expression on page 59 to prepare a short skit between the police officer and Jim. Use the "notes" pages at the back of the book. Start with the following:

Officer: *Good afternoon, sir.*

   Jim: *Good afternoon. I found this envelope on the street.*

Officer: *OK, let me write down some details....*

Practice the dialogue with your partner.
Close your books and practice the skit from memory.

Discussion

Work with another student. Ask and answer the following questions.

1. Which places would you like to visit in China?
2. What do you know about Chinese history and culture?
3. What Chinese food do you like?
4. Who do you usually contact if you are feeling ill?
5. What are the most useful medical items (e.g., band-aids) to keep at home?
6. How do you try to stay healthy?

Online research task

Work in a small group. Do an internet search to find out more about Shanghai. Choose a famous sightseeing spot that interests you.
   • *Watch a YouTube video about it.*
   • *Use Google Maps and an online encyclopedia to learn more.*
   • *Make notes about three things you learned, and share them with another group. Answer their questions using the internet if necessary.*

Example We researched *Yu Garden. It's a famous Chinese garden in the Old City of Shanghai.* We learned three things: *(1) the construction of the garden started in 1559, (2) it covers an area of two hectares, and (3) "Yu" means "pleasing and satisfying to one's parents."*

Self-study

China, paper, and printing

Match the words to the definitions.

1. billion___ 2. subtropical___ 3. consumer___ 4. invention___ 5. originate___ 6. banknote___ 7. movable type___	a) symbols made of metal, wood, etc., from which words and numbers are printed b) money made of paper or similar material c) a thousand million d) bordering on the tropics e) a user of a commodity or service f) something made for the first time g) to begin during a particular period

Listen to the recording and write the answers.

S 34

1. What is the population of Shanghai?
2. What was China's growth rate between 2001 and 2010?
3. How many agricultural workers are there in China?
4. When were banknotes first used?
5. What material was used to make the first banknotes?
6. For what was bronze movable type first used?

Dialogue review

Read through the unit and write answers to the following questions.

1. What kind of internet access did Hana want?
2. When did the hotel restaurant close?
3. List all Hana's symptoms.
4. What did Dr. Chang tell Hana to avoid?
5. What disease did Dr. Chang think Hana had caught?
6. What did Hana order from room service?

Unit 10: Taking a taxi

> **In this unit, you are going to:**
> - study and practice some hotel and taxi conversations
> - practice the phrase *"Roughly ... ?"*
> - discuss museums and art
> - research France

Warm up

Work with another student. Ask and answer the following questions.

1. Describe the photographs.
2. What do you want to know about Paris?
3. What museums would you like to visit in the future, and why?
4. When was the last time you took a taxi? Where did you go?

Museum website

Opening times	Ticket purchased online	Ticket purchased at the museum
9:30am to 6pm	Full rate: €16 ———————	Full rate: €14 Concessional rate: €11
9:30am to 9:45pm on Thursdays	Late opening rate (from 6pm): **€12** Family rate: €13	Late opening rate (from 6pm): €10 Family rate: €11
Closed on Mondays	Under 18s and members: **free**	Under 18s and members: **free**

Carte Blanche Membership	
The Carte Blanche gives unlimited and reserved access to the permanent collections and temporary exhibitions of the Orsay Museum and the Orangerie Museum, as well as many other advantages and discounts for a full year.	€42

Concessions (Discounts)
· for 18 to 25-year-olds who are not citizens or long-term residents of an EU member state · for everyone from 4:30pm (except Thursdays) · for everyone on Thursday evenings, from 6pm

Look at the website information and answer the following questions.

1. If a mother and father decide to take their child to the museum, how much will they pay online?
2. If a French person visits the museum after 6 pm on Thursday and buys a ticket at the museum, how much will she or he pay?
3. What is the advantage of the €42 membership?
4. If a German person visits the museum at 11 am and buys a ticket, how much will she or he pay?
5. If a 21-year-old Japanese person visits the museum at 2 pm and buys a ticket, how much will she or he pay?

Dialogue: **At the hotel**

(S 20 / ○ / T 10)

Listen to the conversation and fill in the blanks.

Hana approaches the receptionist.

Hana Excuse me. Could you help me with some information?

Receptionist Certainly, madam. What would you like to know?

Hana Is the Orsay Museum open today?

Receptionist I'll check the website for you .... Yes, (1)_____.
Are you a citizen or long-term resident of the European Union?

Hana No, I'm visiting from Japan.

Receptionist In that case, you can ask for a concession (2)_____
_____.

Hana Thank you. And where can I get a taxi for the museum?

Receptionist Just outside the hotel.

Hana Roughly (3)_____?

Receptionist From here to the museum, about 15 euros.

Hana Fifty euros – that's expensive!

Receptionist No, no. Fifteen euros. (4)_____. You'll
pay about sixteen euros fifty in total.

Hana Fifteen or sixteen fifty, (5)_____?

Receptionist Usually, we give the driver a tip. About 10 percent.

Hana I see. Thank you.

Receptionist You're welcome.

Now practice the conversation with another student.

Dialogue: **In the taxi**

(S 21 / ○ / T 11)

Listen to the dialogue and answer the following questions.

1. What was the original use of the Orsay Museum building?
2. When is Hana leaving Paris?
3. Where is Hana going?
4. Who is Blek le Rat?

Outside the hotel, Hana gets into a taxi.

Hana Orsay Museum – er, "Musée d' Orsay."

Taxi driver Pardon? Do you speak French?

Hana No, I'm sorry. I don't.

Taxi driver No problem. I can speak English. Where do you want to go?

Hana passes him a piece of paper.

Hana The Orsay Museum.

Taxi driver Ah, the old station.

Hana No, no. The museum. I want to see some paintings.

Taxi driver Ah, it's my joke. The museum building was a railway station. The Orsay station became the Orsay Museum. So, are you on vacation?

Hana For the weekend only. On Monday I'm going to Berlin for a conference.

Taxi driver A Berlin conference. Are you a diplomat?

Hana No, no. I'm a medical student. I'm helping my professor at a medical conference.

Taxi driver Well, please enjoy Paris while you're here. You like art?

Hana Yes. I really want to see the Impressionists.

Taxi driver Monet, Renoir, and the others. But you should also see the pictures of Blek!

Hana Who?

Taxi driver Blek le Rat. He paints the streets.

Hana He paints street scenes?

Taxi driver No, no. He paints on the walls of the streets.

Hana You mean graffiti?

Taxi driver In a way, but Blek is different. I can show you on the way to the museum. It will take us five minutes longer.

Hana <u>Roughly</u> how much more will it cost?

Taxi driver Maybe an extra three euros.

Hana OK. Let's go.

Taxi driver No problem. *Allons-y*!

Now practice the conversation with another student.

Vocabulary check

Read each definition and write down the correct word.

1. a person who lives in a country, city, town, etc.: r_____
2. a reduction in the usual price of a ticket: c_____
3. a government official who works in an embassy: d_____
4. a view of a place or event: s_____
5. a group of objects that have been gathered together by someone: c_____
6. words/pictures written on walls without permission: g_____

Role play

Read through the dialogues. Then close your books and act out the situations.

A: Hana Suzuki

B: receptionist, taxi driver

Key expression: *Roughly ...?*

Hana: Roughly how much more will it cost?

Taxi driver: Maybe an extra three euros.

Work with another student. Ask and answer the questions.

Example

A: Roughly how long does it take to travel from Fukuoka to Tokyo by the fastest train?

B: Let me think ... I guess it takes about five hours by bullet train.

Student A

1. the number of hours **B** spends watching sport in a week (*Roughly how many + do*)
3. the amount of time **B** spends cooking in a month (*Roughly how much + do*)
5. the length of the Amazon River (*Roughly how long + be*)

Student B

2. the number of text messages **A** sends in a day (*Roughly how many + do*)
4. the number of hours **A** spends studying English in a week (*Roughly how many + do*)
6. the distance between Osaka and Tokyo (*Roughly how far + be*)

Dialogue writing

Work with another student. Use the key expression on page 65 to prepare a short skit between Keisuke and Jane, who are planning a barbecue for their art club. They talk about the approximate numbers of people coming, plates, cups, etc.

> *Jane: Hi Keisuke. Shall we start making some plans for the barbecue?*
>
> *Keisuke: OK, let's think about the number of guests, and then plan the food and drink.*
>
> *Jane:*

Practice the dialogue with your partner.
Close your books and practice the skit from memory.

Discussion

Work with another student. Ask and answer the questions.

1. What do you know about France?
2. What famous French people have you heard of?
3. When you think about Paris, what artists and artworks come to mind?
4. If you were in Paris on vacation, what would you do there?
5. What are the good points and bad points about tipping (giving extra money) for service (e.g., to hotel staff)?
6. What French words or phrases do you know? Which ones are used in Japan?

Online research task

Work in a small group. Do an internet search to find out about France. Choose a famous sightseeing spot that interests you.
- *Watch a YouTube video about it.*
- *Use Google maps and an online encyclopedia to learn more.*
- *Make notes about three things you learned, and share them with another group. Answer their questions using the internet if necessary.*

> ***Example*** We researched *the Arc de Triomphe. It's a monument located in the heart of Paris, at the end of the Champs-Élysées.* We learned three things: *(1) It commemorates French military victories, (2) it was commissioned by Napoleon Bonaparte in 1806, and (3) it is the site of the annual military parade on Bastille Day, July 14th.*

Self-study
Paris, the encyclopedia, and painting

Match the words to the definitions.

1. encyclopedia___	a) an educated person interested in ideas and knowledge
2. summarize___	b) to start using a new way of doing something
3. intellectual___	c) a piece of paper/plastic in which shapes have been cut, used for painting on surfaces
4. multiple___	d) ranging from several to many
5. viewpoint___	e) a set of books containing articles on human knowledge
6. stencil___	f) a place from where someone can look at something
7. adopt___	g) to explain key points in a short and clear way

Listen to the recording and write answers to the following questions.
1. What is Paris often called?
2. How many gas lamps were on its streets in the 1860s?
3. What did Diderot and D'Alembert create?
4. Why did many artists come to Paris in the late nineteenth and early twentieth centuries?
5. Which artists created cubism?
6. How and where does Blek le Rat paint his pictures?

S 35

Dialogue review

Read through the unit and answer the following questions.
1. Which museum did Hana want to visit?
2. Roughly how much was the taxi going to cost?
3. What was the original use of the museum building?
4. Why was Hana going to Berlin?
5. What did Hana want to see in the museum?
6. Where does Blek le Rat paint?

Unit 11: At a conference

> **In this unit, you are going to:**
> - study and practice conference-related conversations
> - practice the phrase *"... must be ..."*
> - discuss presentations and speaking in public
> - research Berlin

Warm up

Work with another student. Ask and answer the following questions.

1. Describe the photographs.
2. What would you like to know about Berlin?
3. Which do you prefer, old buildings or modern buildings, and why?
4. Talk about the last time you made a speech or presentation.

Conference location website

Built in 1915, the Langenbeck-Virchow House was reopened on 1 October 2005 following complete restoration and modernization.

Auditorium
Five hundred seats on the main floor and in the gallery can now be used for meetings and other events. The auditorium is fitted with the very latest technical equipment, including state-of-the-art media technology for live transmissions of national and international events.

Foyer
The spacious foyer can be used for many different purposes – the ideal setting for everything from coffee breaks to evening events. Our in-house caterer will take care of the eating and drinking arrangements for your event.

Conference and seminar rooms
The Langenbeck-Virchow House also offers excellent possibilities for smaller scale events. Our two seminar rooms are fully equipped technically and can accommodate various sized groups:
- "Bernhard von Langenbeck" seminar room (approx. 50–90 people)
- "Rudolf Virchow" conference room (approx. 30–60 people)

These numbers can be adjusted based on the seating arrangements required.
If necessary and subject to availability, further seminar rooms can be rented.

Look at the website information and answer the following questions.

1. When was the Langenbeck-Virchow House reopened?
2. What would be the best place for giving a presentation to 25 people?
3. What would be the best place for giving a presentation to 325 people?
4. Who takes care of the food and drink for a conference at the Langenbeck-Virchow House?
5. Which area is good for buffet lunches?

Dialogue: At the conference reception desk

Listen to the conversation and fill in the blanks.

Hana approaches the receptionist.

Receptionist Could I have your name, please?

Hana It's Suzuki – Hana Suzuki.

Receptionist One moment .... Ah, here it is. (1) _____, and your conference pack.

Hana Thank you. And (2)_____?

Receptionist Actually we don't. It's a fairly small building. The party this evening will be here in the foyer, and the coffee breaks, lunches, and poster presentations will also take place here. The three conference presentation rooms are upstairs. Oh, and (3)_____ _____ from Professor Mori.

Hana (4) _____?

Receptionist Unfortunately, he has appendicitis and can't come.

Hana Oh, no!

Receptionist (5)_____to say that you will make the presentation for him, so it hasn't been canceled.

Hana Thank you for telling me.

Receptionist You're welcome.

Now practice the conversation with another student.

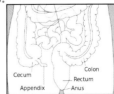

Dialogue: At the conference party

Listen to the dialogue and answer the following questions.

1. Where is David Matthews from?
2. Where is Kurt Ritter from?
3. Where and when is Hana's presentation?
4. Where is Hana staying?

Hana gets a drink from the bar. Another conference participant is also getting a drink. He turns to Hana.

Doctor 1 Orange juice? You <u>must be</u> presenting early tomorrow!

   Hana Actually, you're right. I am!

Doctor 1 I'm David Matthews from Bart's in London. (*They shake hands.*)

   Hana I'm Hana Suzuki from Hiroshima University. You said "Bars"?

Doctor 1 St. Bartholomew's Hospital in London – "Bart's" for short. What's your specialism?

   Hana Actually, I'm a medical student. I was meant to be assisting Dr. Mori, but he's got appendicitis.

Doctor 1 Oh, I know Dr. Mori. But he's an appendix specialist! (*Another doctor approaches.*) Oh, hello Kurt. I thought you'd be here. (*They shake hands.*) Good to see you. This is Hana Suzuki, a medical student from Hiroshima. (*Hana and Kurt shake hands.*)

Doctor 2 Hello Hana. I'm Kurt Ritter from the University Medical Center, Hamburg.

Doctor 1 Dr. Mori's got appendicitis, so Hana here has to give the presentation.

   Hana Yes, I'm very nervous about it.

Doctor 2 Do you have the presentation notes and the slides?

   Hana Yes, I worked on them with Dr. Mori and an English specialist.

Doctor 2 And did you work on the research with Dr. Mori?

   Hana Yes, I did.

Doctor 2 Well, don't worry. You can explain about Dr. Mori at the beginning of the presentation. The audience will understand. What time are you making it and where?

   Hana At 9:00 in the seminar room.

Doctor 2 The first presentation – that's good. I know Takashi – Dr. Mori. We're in the same field. I'll come along tomorrow. If you have any problems with questions, give me a signal and I'll help. If I were you, I'd go to the seminar room early to set up.

   Hana That's a good idea. It's only a fifteen-minute walk from the conference hotel to here, so I can do that.

Doctor 2 I think most of us are staying there, so we may see you at breakfast tomorrow. (*He turns to Doctor 1.*) So, David. How is Bart's? ...

Now practice the conversation with another student.

— 70 —

Vocabulary check

Read each definition and write down the correct word.

1. a person who provides food for an event: c_____
2. a meeting where an expert talks with a small group: s_____
3. a small label worn to show that you are a member of a group: b_____
4. a large open area just inside the entrance of a public building: f_____
5. a medical condition due to an infected appendix: a_____
6. a group of people who listen to or watch an event: a_____

Role play

Read through the dialogues. Then close your books and act out the situations.

A: Hana Suzuki
B: receptionist, Doctor 1, Doctor 2

Key expression: ... *must be* ...

Doctor 1: Orange juice? You must be presenting early tomorrow!
   Hana: Actually, you're right. I am!

Work with another student. Listen to the information and give a response.

Example
A: Tom had to work until 2:00 am.
B: Wow, that's late! He must be tired.

Student A
1. I have my driving test tomorrow.
3. Tomoyo ran in a 90 km race last month.
5. Ken and Sam had to skip lunch because of the meeting.

Student B
2. Bill and Molly haven't had anything to drink for the last six hours.
4. Keisuke can lift 100 kg in the gym.
6. I studied English until 3:00 am this morning.

Dialogue writing

Work with another student. Emi is attending an international student conference in Munich and arrived from Japan in the afternoon. She is going to make a presentation. At the conference party in the evening, she meets Erika, a student from Vienna. Use the key expression on page 71 to prepare a short skit.

> **Erika:** *Hi, I'm Erika.*
>   **Emi:** *Oh hi, I'm Emi. I'm from Fukuoka University.*
> **Erika:** *Fuku ...?*
>   **Emi:**

Practice the dialogue with your partner.
Close your books and practice the skit from memory.

Discussion

Work with another student. Ask and answer the questions.

1. Talk about the last time you were very nervous.
2. Do you like speaking in public? Why or why not?
3. What do you do to prepare for a speech or presentation?
4. What would you like to research in the future, and why?
5. What do you know about Germany and German culture?
6. If you went to Germany, what would you do there?

Online research task

Work in a small group. Do an internet search to find out about Berlin. Choose a famous sightseeing spot that interests you.
- *Watch a YouTube video about the place.*
- *Use Google maps and an online encyclopedia to learn more about it.*
- *Make notes about three things you learned, and share them with another group. Answer their questions using the internet if necessary.*

> ***Example*** We researched *the Brandenburg Gate. It is one of Berlin's most important monuments.* We learned three things: *(1) It was built in the late eighteenth century, (2) its design is neoclassical, and (3) it changed from a symbol of the division between East and West Berlin to one of unity after the fall of the Berlin Wall.*

Self-study
Berlin and the Wall

Match the words to the definitions.

1. high-tech___	a) relating to the way a country or area is governed
2. communist___	b) a place where people are stopped and asked questions, often at a border
3. politically___	c) a person who is not a member of the police or armed forces
4. authorities___	d) using the most advanced machines and processes
5. checkpoint___	e) following principles in which all production and property is owned by the state on behalf of the people
6. civilian___	f) institutions with the power to make decisions and enforce laws, such as the government and police
7. reunify___	g) to become one again after being divided

Listen to the recording and write answers to the following questions.

1. What is the population of Berlin?
2. What was the capital city of West Germany?
3. What was the capital city of East Germany?
4. What did the East German authorities start to do in 1961?
5. What was the name of the best known checkpoint?
6. What happened in October 1990?

Dialogue review

Read through the unit and answer the following questions.

1. What was wrong with Dr. Mori?
2. Where was the party?
3. What is "Bart's"?
4. Who worked on the presentation notes and slides?
5. What did Kurt Ritter say he would do?
6. How far was the conference hotel from the conference site?

Unit 12: Conference presentation

> **In this unit, you are going to:**
> - study and practice some hotel and seminar room conversations
> - practice *"I have a problem (with) ..."*
> - discuss architecture and issues with technology at conferences
> - research Germany

Warm up

Work with another student. Ask and answer the following questions.

1. Describe the photographs.
2. Which of the two buildings in the photographs do you prefer, and why?
3. What do you use your computer for?
4. When was the last time someone helped you with a problem?

Museum information

OPENING HOURS
Daily 10 am to 6 pm
Closed 24 December

ADMISSION
Free up to 18 years
Day ticket for all exhibitions: €10, reduced* €5
Annual ticket €50 (with accompanying person €70), reduced* €40

FEE FOR GUIDED TOURS
€3 plus admission, children €2
Family ticket €18 (admission plus guided tour for 2 adults and max. 3 children)
Groups €75 (for up to 25 participants plus entrance fee)
Groups €30 (for up to 10 participants plus entrance fee)
Student groups €1 (per student)

TOUR BOOKING
Permanent exhibition Tel. +49 30 20304-751
Special exhibitions Tel. +49 30 20304-750
Fax +49 30 20304-759 fuehrung@dhm.de

* Discount applicable for pupils and people in apprenticeship over 18 years, students, unemployed, and disabled persons.

Look at the website information and answer the following questions.

1. What would Hana pay for a museum ticket?
2. How much would a husband, wife, and two children pay for a guided tour?
3. What would it cost for three sixteen-year-olds to go round the museum?
4. How many hours is the museum open on a normal day?
5. What letters show that an email address is German?

Dialogue: **At breakfast**

Listen to the conversation and fill in the blanks.

Hana enters the hotel restaurant.

    Hana Good morning.

Manager Good morning. (1)_____?

    Hana It's Suzuki, room number 311.

Manager Thank you. The breakfast buffet is just over there. (2)_____

_____.

As Hana walks into the breakfast area, she sees Dr. Ritter, who is reading a paper at a window table. She goes over to him.

    Hana Good morning, Dr. Ritter.

    Kurt Ah, good morning. We are the early ones. (3)_____

_____?

    Hana Thank you.

Hana puts down her computer bag, gets some coffee and a roll, then returns to the table.

    Kurt So, are you ready for the presentation?

    Hana (4)_____. I have my handouts ready, and I have the presentation slides on a USB.

    Kurt May I have one of the handouts?

    Hana Sure. Here you are, and here's a copy of the presentation notes.

    Kurt Ah, thank you. That's very helpful. I'll read these quickly after breakfast, and I'll come to the seminar room around 8:40. At least you can relax after this morning.

    Hana Yes, that's true. If I can get through today, I'm going to do some sightseeing tomorrow afternoon for a few hours. I want to visit the German Historical Museum and Museum Island. (5)_____?

    Kurt I may stroll up to Robert-Koch-Platz to see the statue of Dr. Koch. He's a hero of mine.

Now practice the conversation with another student.

Dialogue: **In the seminar room**

Listen to the dialogue and answer the following questions.

1. What problem does Hana have?
2. What does Kurt suggest that Hana do?
3. How do Hana and Kurt finally solve the problem?
4. Where is Kurt going to sit?

Hana is in the seminar room struggling with the computer. Kurt enters.

Kurt Are you OK?

Hana No, not really. <u>I have a problem</u> opening my presentation file.

Kurt Is it on the desktop?

Hana No, it's on the USB, but it won't open.

Kurt How about copying it to the desktop and trying to open it from there?

Hana copies the file onto the desktop and tries to open it again.

Hana No, it still won't open.

Kurt May I try? Is it a Windows or a Mac file?

Hana It's a Mac file.

Kurt Well, it certainly won't open!

Hana I'll go get some help.

Hana leaves the seminar room, goes down to the foyer, and sees a conference helper.

Hana Excuse me, <u>I have a problem with</u> the presentation software in the seminar room. Can you help me?

Helper Sure.

They return to the seminar room. Kurt is still struggling with the computer.

Hana Any luck?

Kurt No, I still can't get it open.

Helper Have you copied the file to the desktop?

Hana Yes, we have. It's a Mac file. Is that a problem?

Helper It shouldn't be. I'll have to find a technician.

Kurt We're running out of time. Hana, are you carrying your own computer?

Hana Yes.

Kurt Can we hook up her computer?

Helper Yes, you can attach it to this lead.

Kurt Let's do it.

They hook up Hana's computer. The first slide appears on the screen.

Hana That's great! Thank you so much, Dr. Ritter.

Kurt You're welcome. I'll sit there on the edge of the front row. Good luck with the presentation!

Now practice the conversation with another student.

Vocabulary check

Read each definition and write down the correct word.

1. a reduction in the price of something: d_____
2. a meal where people serve themselves: b_____
3. a stone or bronze figure of a person or animal: s_____
4. to move a file from a storage device onto a computer: c_____
5. a small data storage device: U_____
6. to connect equipment using a cable or lead: h_____ u_____

Role play

Read through the dialogues. Then close your books and act out the situations.

A: Hana Suzuki
B: Kurt Ritter, helper

Key expression: *I have a problem* (*with*) ...

Kurt: Are you OK?
Hana: No, not really. I have a problem opening my presentation file.
Kurt: Is it on the desktop?
Hana: No, it's on a USB, but it won't open.
Kurt: How about copying it onto the desktop and trying to open it from there?

Work with another student. Listen to the problem and make suggestions.

Example
A: I have a problem with my car. It won't start.
B: Maybe it'll start if we get it moving. Shall we give it a push?
A: OK. Let's try it. Thanks.

Student A
1. Your club activities are affecting your studies.
3. You can't get any reception on your smartphone.
5. Your air-conditioner doesn't keep your room cool.

Student B
2. Your boss often shouts at you.
4. You are often late for class.
6. The TV remote control isn't working.

Dialogue writing

Work with another student. Kana's boss wants her to work late every evening. She meets her friend, Jim, talks about the problem, and Jim gives advice. Use the key expression on page 77 and prepare a short skit.

> **Jim:** *Hi Kana. You seem a bit down. Is anything wrong?*
>
> **Kana:** *I'm upset about my part-time job.*
>
> **Jim:** *Sometimes it helps to talk. Can you tell me about it?*
>
> **Kana:**

Practice the dialogue with your partner.
Close your books and practice the skit from memory.

Discussion

Work with another student. Ask and answer the questions.

1. Have you ever had a computer problem? What was it and what did you do?
2. What software programs do you use? Which is the most useful for you?
3. When was the last time you helped someone with a minor problem?
4. Which is more useful, a smartphone or a laptop computer, and why?
5. Which do you prefer, USBs or cloud storage, and why?
6. What do you do to relax after a stressful day?

Online research task

Work in a small group. Do an internet search to find out about Germany. Choose a famous sightseeing spot that is not in Berlin.

- *Watch a YouTube video about the place.*
- *Use Google maps and an online encyclopedia to learn more about it.*
- *Make notes about three things you learned, and share them with another group. Answer their questions using the internet if necessary.*

> ***Example*** We researched *Neuschwanstein Castle in Bavaria.* We learned three things: *(1) It was built by King Ludwig II of Bavaria in the late nineteenth century, (2) its stunning architecture and beautiful location in the Bavarian Alps has attracted many musicians and writers, and (3) its design was the main inspiration for Walt Disney's Cinderella Castle.*

Self-study
The Bauhaus and Modernism

Match the words to the definitions.

1. eclectic___	a) a situation in which sounds, colors, or objects match each other
2. fine arts___	b) the effect that someone or something has on people or events
3. crafts___	c) relating to where people live
4. influence___	d) someone living in the same period as someone else
5. harmony___	e) varied, without a main idea
6. contemporary___	f) the art of planning and decorating the inside of buildings
7. residential___	g) painting and sculpture
8. interior design___	h) artistic activities for making functional items

Listen to the recording and write answers to the following questions.
1. When did the Weimar Republic start and end?
2. What did the Bauhaus school combine?
3. What did the Bauhaus style focus on?
4. What did Bruno Taut and Ernst May build?
5. When did the Bauhaus school close?
6. What did many architects and designers do after 1933?

Dialogue review

Read through the unit and answer the following questions.
1. What did Hana give Kurt at breakfast?
2. What places was Hana planning to see in Berlin?
3. Was Hana using a Windows or a Mac file?
4. Who did Hana find in the foyer?
5. What was the problem with finding a technician?
6. How was Hana able to open the file?

Review Section of Units 7-12

1. *Look at units 7 to 12 and choose three units. What problem did Hana have in the units you have chosen?*

Unit （　　　　）：_____

_____

Unit （　　　　）：_____

_____

Unit （　　　　）：_____

_____

2. *How did she solve the problems in those three units?*

Unit （　　　　）：_____

_____

Unit （　　　　）：_____

_____

Unit （　　　　）：_____

_____

3. *With a partner, choose one unit. Read the second dialogue aloud by yourself. Then practice the conversation with your partner.*

4. *Close your books and role-play the conversation.*

5. *Choose one of Hana's journeys below and write a summary of it with a title. Use the "notes" pages at the back of the book for the summary.*

   a. Delhi, Agra, Bangkok, and Shanghai

   b. Paris and Berlin

Read your partner's summary and write some comments and questions.

6. *Choose one of Hana's experiences from Units 7 to 12 and present (1) a summary of it to the class with a focus on the problem and how she solved it along with (2) your personal reflection on the topic. Prepare visuals using PowerPoint or other software for your presentation. Use the past tense when writing your script. Use your own words to present the summary.*

Example: *(1) I am going to talk about Hana's trip from Delhi to Agra. She booked a bus tour, and she had to wait near the hotel reception desk for the tour guide to pick her up. ... On the tour bus a young man was very thirsty and had a headache, so Hana ....*
(2) Now, let me share my thoughts. I think taking a guided tour by bus is very convenient. ... The young man was very lucky that Hana was so well prepared ....

Listen to the presentions and write questions you want to ask.

Self-Study Listening: Texts

1. Singapore

The Republic of Singapore is a modern city state in Southeast Asia. Its name comes from a Malay word that means "Lion City." It has a mixed population of almost six million people. The biggest ethnic group is Chinese. Other significant ethnic groups are Malays and Indians. There are four official languages in Singapore: English, Malay, Mandarin Chinese, and Tamil.

Because of Singapore's important strategic location, Stamford Raffles created a trading post for the British East India Company on the island, which quickly grew into a major port for trade. For many years the island was under British control.

Singapore became an independent republic in 1965, and is now one of the world's major commercial hubs. It has one of the largest financial centers in the world, and its port is one of the busiest. It is a major oil-refining center, a producer of oil-rigs, and a major hub for ship repair services. It is also an important producer of semiconductors, and it has a large tourism industry.

2. London and the Greenwich Observatory

London is the capital city of both England and the United Kingdom. It is a leading global city, with a reputation in sectors such as education, entertainment, fashion, finance, tourism, and the arts. London has four World Heritage Sites. One of these is Maritime Greenwich. In Greenwich, the Royal Observatory is the home of Greenwich Mean Time and the Prime Meridian line.

The Royal Observatory was founded by Charles II in 1675. As England was a major trading nation, navigation at sea was of vital importance. The Royal Observatory was built to improve navigation at sea and find a solution to the problem of longitude: For sailors, it was difficult to find their exact position east and west while at sea.

In 1714, the British parliament offered a huge reward to anyone who could solve the problem of finding longitude at sea. The prize was finally won by a clockmaker, John Harrison. Harrison's chronometer H4 changed navigation forever. British sailors kept at least one chronometer running on the time at Greenwich (Greenwich Mean Time) to calculate their longitude from the Greenwich Meridian, which was given a longitude of zero degrees. This system was internationally adopted in 1884.

3. Edinburgh and the Enlightenment

Edinburgh is the capital city of Scotland, with a population of around 550,000 people. It is the second most popular city for tourism in the United Kingdom after

London.

In the eighteenth century, the city was called "the Athens of the North." This was partly due to the design of some of its main buildings, but mainly because of its reputation for learning. Edinburgh was at the center of the "the Scottish Enlightenment." The Enlightenment was a key period in Europe, in which reason and science were emphasized as ways of understanding and explaining the world. An example of an Enlightenment thinker is Adam Smith, who spent part of his life in Edinburgh. He is often called "the father of economics." His two main written works are "The Theory of Moral Sentiments," in which he wrote about how people come to make moral judgements, and "The Wealth of Nations," in which he discussed the development and organization of countries' economies in the early years of the Industrial Revolution.

Modern-day Edinburgh is well known for its financial services sector, scientific research, higher education, and tourism. A third of all office space in the city is used for financial services. Two central areas of Edinburgh, the Old Town and the New Town, together form a UNESCO World Heritage Site. Every year in August, the Edinburgh Festival is held, in which various organizations and groups produce shows and events in the city.

S 29

4. Canada

Canada is a country of ten provinces and three territories. It extends from the Atlantic Ocean to the Pacific Ocean and northward into the Arctic Ocean. It covers an area of 9.98 million square kilometers. This makes it the world's second-largest country by total area and the fourth-largest country by land area. Canada's border with the United States is the world's longest land border.

Canada is a federal parliamentary democracy and a constitutional monarchy. King Charles III is the current head of state. The country has two official languages: English and French. It is one of the world's most ethnically diverse and multicultural nations. This is because of large-scale immigration from many countries. It has a population of over 38 million.

Since the early 20th century, the growth of Canada's manufacturing, mining, and service sectors has changed its economy. Like many other developed nations, the Canadian economy has a very large service sector, which employs about three-quarters of the country's workforce. However, Canada is unusual among developed countries because of the importance of its primary sector. The logging and petroleum industries are two of the biggest in this sector.

It is one of the few developed nations that exports more energy than it imports. Atlantic Canada has huge amounts of natural gas, and Alberta also has large oil and gas resources. The Athabasca oil sands and other sources of oil result in

Canada having around 10% of global oil reserves. This is the world's third-largest share after Venezuela and Saudi Arabia. Canada is also one of the world's largest exporters of agricultural products such as wheat.

S 30

5. The USA and the American Revolution

The United States of America consists of 50 states and the federal district of Washington D.C. It has a population of around 340 million, the third largest in the world after India and China. In terms of area, it covers 9.8 million square kilometers. It is a constitutional republic and representative democracy, and is the world's oldest surviving federation. The federal government has three branches: The legislative branch consists of the Senate and the House of Representatives, the executive branch consists of the President and members of his or her cabinet, and the judicial branch consists of the Supreme Court and lower federal courts.

The United States emerged from 13 British colonies located along the East Coast of North America. Disputes between Great Britain and the 13 colonies led to the American Revolution. War started in April 1775 and ended in 1783 with the defeat of a British army at Yorktown.

On July 4, 1776, delegates from the 13 colonies adopted the Declaration of Independence. At the beginning of the document, it stated that that "all men are created equal" and that they had various rights including rights to "Life, Liberty, and the pursuit of Happiness." It went on to state that those rights were not being protected by Great Britain, and declared that the thirteen colonies were independent states. The fourth of July is celebrated annually as Independence Day.

S 31

6. Aviation in the USA

The United States has a long history of aviation, from the first powered flights to the development of passenger jets. Two of the most famous figures in aviation are the brothers Wilbur and Orville Wright. The two brothers had a bicycle business, and used the profits from this to design and build aircraft. They felt that flying an aircraft had the same challenges as riding a bicycle, requiring constant adjustments to maintain control. This was in comparison to the stability of cars. Consequently, they thought carefully about how a pilot needed to control an aircraft. After making efficient gliders, the brothers wanted to make an airplane with an engine. They built the airplane, named Flyer 1, using spruce, a very strong light wood, and covered the wings and tail in fabric. Their bicycle shop mechanic Charlie Taylor built a light engine using aluminum, which they fixed to the plane. They first flew the airplane in 1903.

One of the most famous American companies in the history of aviation is the Boeing Corporation. Its founder was William E. Boeing, who based the company in

Seattle. This was partly because of the spruce forests near the city. The first plane that the company built was a seaplane called the Boeing Model 1. Over the decades, Boeing produced aircraft both for military and commercial use.

Perhaps the most famous of the Boeing aircraft is the Boeing 747. The boss of Pan Am, Juan Trippe, and the president of Boeing, Bill Allen, wanted to build an airplane that could carry twice as many passengers as any other airplane. Trippe ordered twenty-five of the new planes in order to make the project possible, and so Boeing built a huge factory just north of Seattle. The 747s went into service in 1970 and became a great commercial success for Boeing. Due to the passenger capacity of the 747s, airlines were able to lower the prices of their tickets, making airplane travel possible for more people than ever before.

S 32

7. India, spices, cotton, and Gandhi

In 2023, with over 1.4 billion people, the Republic of India's population overtook that of China. It is the seventh-largest country by area, and has one of the fastest growing economies. Fifty-four percent of its GDP comes from the service sector, 26 percent from the industrial sector, and 20 percent from the agricultural sector. India has the second-largest smartphone market after China.

Historically, India was involved in large amounts of foreign trade. This was due to its importance as a producer of spices. The most important of these was pepper, produced in large quantities in the Kerala region. It was bought by Arab traders and entered Europe through the markets in Venice. However, after the Portuguese explorer Vasco de Gama sailed round Africa and then to India, most trade went by this sea route, with European countries competing against each other. With the rise in power of the British East India Company, India gradually came under its control, and then became a colony of the British Empire. Another important Indian agricultural product was cotton. As Britain began to industrialize, large amounts of cotton were shipped to cotton mills in the north of England and a lot of the cloth made in Britain was then sold in India.

In 1947 India became an independent republic. A key figure in the independence movement was Mohandas Gandhi. After returning to India in 1915, Gandhi soon started to reject western clothing and became famous for non-violent campaigns against unfair land tax and discrimination. He encouraged Indians to stop buying imported cloth from Britain, and to use small spinning wheels to spin their own cotton. In 1930, Gandhi walked to the sea to make salt in order to campaign against a salt tax. He also worked to improve the position of women and low-status workers in Indian society. He was given the name "Mahatma," which means "Great Soul," and was also called "Bapu," which means "Father."

8. Thailand and Bangkok

Thailand is a located in Mainland Southeast Asia. It has land borders with Myanmar, Laos, Cambodia, and Malaysia. It has a total area of approximately 513,000 square kilometers, and a population of around 70 million people. The main religion is Buddhism. Major sectors of the economy are manufacturing and agriculture, as well as tourism. Thailand is one of the most visited countries in Southeast Asia.

Thailand had rapid economic growth between 1985 and 1996, becoming a newly industrialized country and a major exporter. Its main industries include electric appliances, computer components, and vehicles.

About 30 percent of Thailand's labor force is employed in agriculture. Rice is the most important crop in the country, and Thailand is one of the world's leading exporters of rice along with India and Vietnam.

Bangkok is the capital of Thailand and its largest city, with a population of over eight million. It is Thailand's political, commercial, industrial, and cultural hub. Many multinational corporations have their regional headquarters in Bangkok. The city is now a major regional force in finance and business. It is an international hub for transport and healthcare, and it is a regional center for the arts, fashion, and entertainment. Bangkok is among the world's top tourist destinations.

9. China, paper, and printing

With over 1.4 billion people, China has the second-largest population in the world. Beijing, its capital city, has a population of around 22 million, and Shanghai, with a population of approximately 25 million, is the largest city in the world. China has one of the world's largest land areas, covering an area of around 9.6 million square kilometers. It contains very varied landscapes ranging from deserts to subtropical forests.

China has been one of the fastest growing major economies. Between 2001 and 2010 its average growth rate was 10.5 percent. It is the world's largest manufacturing economy, and Shanghai has the world's busiest container port. China is also the world's largest producer and consumer of agricultural products. Around 22 percent of the workforce are involved in agriculture. China is the world's largest producer of rice.

China has a long cultural history, and is linked to many inventions; for example, banknotes were first used in China around 118 BC. At that time, they were made from leather. Paper is another Chinese invention. Cai Lun is traditionally regarded as the inventor of the papermaking process, although early forms of paper existed in the second century BC. Copper movable type printing was also invented in China at the beginning of the twelfth century and was used for printing paper money.

10. Paris, the encyclopedia, and painting

France is a republic with a population of 68 million people. The capital is Paris, which has an area of 105.4 square kilometers and a population of over two million people within its city limits. It is often called the "the city of light." This is for two reasons. One is that it was the first European city to use gas street lighting. In the 1860s, it had 56,000 gas lamps on its streets. The other more important reason is because of its leading role during the Enlightenment. An example of this was Diderot and D'Alembert's creation of an encyclopedia, which was based on human reason. It was a project to collect and summarize human knowledge. Many of the French intellectuals of that time, such as Voltaire, Rousseau, and Montesquieu, wrote articles for the encyclopedia.

Paris was a leading city for fine art in the nineteenth and early twentieth century. Many artists came to Paris to paint and to show their paintings and sculptures. Monet is one of the impressionists associated with the city, and many of his paintings can be seen in the Orsay Museum and in the Orangerie Museum. The artists Pablo Picasso and George Braque created cubism, in which objects are drawn from multiple viewpoints. Henri Matisse is associated with Fauvism, with its bright colors and strong brush strokes. An example of more recent artwork in Paris is the street art of Blek Le Rat, who uses stencils and spray paint to create pictures on the walls and buildings of Paris. His approach to street art was adopted by London artists such as Banksy.

11. Berlin and the Wall

Germany is a federal parliamentary republic. With 84 million people, it has the largest population and the largest economy in the European Union. Berlin, with a population of 3.7 million, is Germany's capital city. About one third of Berlin's area consists of forests, parks, gardens, rivers, and lakes. Its economy has both high-tech industries and services. It is also famous for art and culture.

After World War II, Germany was divided into two countries: West Germany, whose capital city was Bonn, and East Germany, whose capital city was East Berlin. Although West Berlin was politically part of liberal-democratic West Germany, it was located in communist East Germany.

In 1961, the East German authorities started to build a wall around West Berlin, stopping people from freely moving between the two parts of the city. To travel from one side of the wall to the other, they had to pass through checkpoints. The best known of these was Checkpoint Charlie.

On 9th November 1989, under pressure from the civilian population, and with large crowds at the checkpoints, the East German authorities began to allow free movement between East Berlin and West Berlin. A group of young people from

West Berlin jumped onto the wall and were joined by a group from East Berlin. The following year, Germany was reunified, and Berlin became its capital city.

12. The Bauhaus and Modernism

Berlin's history has left the city with an eclectic mix of architecture. The city's appearance in the 21st century has been shaped by the key role the city played in Germany's 20th-century history. One of the most interesting periods was during the Weimar Republic, which lasted from 1919 to 1933.

In the 1920s and early 1930s Germany had a strong reputation for modern design and architecture. The Bauhaus school combined crafts with fine arts, and became famous for its approach to design, with students learning the basic principles of design and color theory, then experimenting with a range of materials and processes. The Bauhaus had a big influence on later developments in art, architecture, graphic design, interior design, and industrial design. The Bauhaus style focused on harmony between the function of an object or a building and its design.

Although the Bauhaus had a great impact on design, it was the Bauhaus contemporaries such as Bruno Taut and Ernst May who built the thousands of residential buildings in Germany at that time. Such architects wished to improve the quality of life for ordinary Germans by creating low-cost apartments with functional spaces and light.

With the rise to power of the Nazis in 1933, the Bauhaus school closed. Many famous architects and designers, including Walter Gropius (the founder of the Bauhaus school) and Bruno Taut, left Germany. They continued their work in other parts of the world. The ideas of such modernists were a major influence on architecture and design in the twentieth century.

Notes

Photographs

Bullet trains p.3 By Walter Davies
Bus p.3 By Walter Davies
Streetcar p.3 Walter Davies
JAL plane p.3 By Sergey Kustov /CC BY-SA 3.0
Subway p.3 By Lover of Romance/CC BY-SA-3.0
Train p.3 By Walter Davies
Taxi p.3 By Walter Davies
Bicycle p.3 By Walter Davies
Mt Fuji p.4 By Shutterstock
Big Buddha p.4 By Shutterstock
Singapore Marina Bay day view p. 6 By Shutterstock
Merlion and Marina Bay Towers night view p.6 By Shutterstock
Prohibited items p.7 By Singapore airlines
Airplane interior p.8 By Shutterstock
Singapore container port p.11 By Shutterstock
London View p.12 By Shutterstock
British Museum p.12 By Shutterstock
Ticket machines p.14 By Walter Davies
Train p.14 By Walter Davies
Greenwich Royal Observatory p.17 By Kjetil Bjørnsrud/CC BY-SA-3.0
Greenwich panorama p.17 By Bill Bertram/CC BY-SA 3.0
H4 p.17 By Phantom Photographer/CC BY-SA 3.0
Cutty Sark p.17 By Gordon Joly/CC BY-SA 3.0
View towards Edinburgh Castle p.18 By Shutterstock
Old College of Edinburgh University p.18 By Shutterstock
Student room p.18 By Edinburgh University
Student living area p.18 By Edinburgh University
Haggis, neeps and tatties p.20 By Shutterstock
Pint of beer p.20 GeoTrinity, CC BY-SA 3.0
Fish and chips p.20 By Shutterstock
Statue of David Hume p.23 By Shutterstock
National Gallery of Scotland p.23 By Shutterstock
Statue of Adam Smith p.23 By Shutterstock
Aerial view of Vancouver p.24 By Shutterstock
Bears p.23 By Koji Uenishi
Cat p.26 By Simon Fraser
Shower p.25 Cat p.23 By Simon Fraser
Wheat p.28 By Bluemoose CC BY-SA-3.0
Mountie p.28 By HordeFTL/public domain
Oil Sands p.28 By Georgialh/CC BY-SA 3.0
Banff mountains p.28 By Tobias Alt,Tobi 87/CC BY-SA 4.0-3.0-2.5-2.0-1.0
Greyhound bus p.30 By SounderBruce, CC BY-SA 2.0
Peace Arch p.30 By Shutterstock
Cup of coffee p.31 By Walter Davies
Passport p.32 By Walter Davies
Star Spangled Banner p.34 By Smithsonian Institution Archives/public domain
Declaration of Independence p.34 By John Trumbull/public domain
Washington Crossing the Delaware p.34 By Emanuel Leutze/public domain
View of Seattle and Mt. Rainier p.36 By Shutterstock
Airplanes at the Museum of Flight p.36 By Shutterstock

Flight Simulator p.38 The Museum of Flight
Wilbur Wright p.41 By Orville Wright and Wilbur Wright (credited as photographers)/ public domain
Orville Wright p.41 By Orville Wright and Wilbur Wright (credited as photographers)/ public domain
Wrights' bicycle p.41 By 350z33/CC BY-SA 3.0
Flyer 1 p.41 By Wright brothers (OhioLINK Digital Media Center)/public domain
Boeing 747 p.41 By Eduard Marmet/ CC BY-SA-3.0
Taj Mahal p.44 By Shutterstock
Agra Fort p.44 By Shutterstock
Bottles of water p.46 By Walter Davies
Aspirin p.46 By Walter Davies
Growing pepper p.49 By K Hari Krishnan/CC BY-SA 3.0
Black pepper p.49 By Walter Davies
Gandhi p.49 Unknown/public domain
Cotton p.49 By CSIRO/ CC BY-SA 3.0
Bangkok and Grand Palace p.50 By Shutterstock
Temple of Dawn p.50 By By Shutterstock
Tuk Tuk p.50 By Ilya Plekhanov/CC BY-SA 3.0
Pickup Truck p.50 By Shutterstock
Keys p.52 Walter Davies
Statue p.55 By Axel Harting
Ceremony p.55 By John Shedrick/CC BY-SA 2.0
Rice planting p.55 By Chiba007CC BY-SA-3.0
Boats p.55 By smmohsinnaseem/CC BY-SA 3.0
Shanghai cityscape p.56 By Shutterstock
Shanghai traditional suburb p.56 By Shutterstock
Great Wall p.61 By Bjoern Kriewald/Public domain
River view p.61 By Charlie Fong/Public domain
Container ship p.61 By Shutterstock
Old banknote p.60 By Jin dynasty government/public domain
Paris and the Eiffel Tower p.62 By Shutterstock
Arc de Triomphe p.62 By Shutterstock
Orsay Museum p.63 By Shadowgate/CC BY 2.0
Orsay Station p.64 Unknown/CC BY-SA 3.0
Orsay Museum p.64 By Shutterstock
Blek le Rat picture p.64 By Shutterstock
Cubist picture p.67 By Tadeusz Makowski/public domain
Impressionist picture p.67 By Claude Monet/public domain
Fauvist picture p.67 By Alexis Mérodack-Jeanneau (1873-1919)/Public domain
View of Berlin p.68 By Shutterstock
Brandenberg Gate p.68 By Shutterstock
Appendix diagram p.69 By William Crochot/public domain
L-V House interior p.69 By the Langenbeck-Virchow House
Drinks p.70 By Walter Davies
Langenbeck-Virchow House By Marek Śliwecki, CC BY-SA 4.0
West and East Germany p.73 By Shutterstock
Berlin Wall p.73 By Axel Harting
Crowd on the Berlin Wall p.73 Lear 21/CC BY-SA 3.0
Alte Nationalgalerie p.74 By Shutterstock
Neue Nationalgalerie p. 74 By Shutterstock
Robert Koch statue p.75 By OTFW/ CC BY-SA 3.0

English for Exploring the World
— Developing Communication Skills
エクスプロアリング・ザ・ワールド

2024年1月15日　初　版

著　　者 ©　Koji Uenishi
　　　　　　Walter Davies
　　　　　　Simon Fraser
　　　　　　Julia Tanabe
　　　　　　Daniel Hougham

発 行 者　　佐 々 木　　元

発 行 所　　株式会社　英 宝 社

〒 101-0032　東京都千代田区岩本町 2-7-7
☎ [03] (5833) 5870　Fax [03] (5833) 5872

ISBN 978-4-269-66059-5 C1082
印刷・製本：モリモト印刷株式会社